Secrets of Xuan Kong
玄空秘旨

an English translation with commentaries

by
Hung Hin Cheong

SECRETS OF XUAN KONG

Published in Kuala Lumpur, Malaysia by JY Books Sdn. Bhd. (659134-T)

Text © Hung Hin Cheong 2011
Design and illustrations © JY Books Sdn. Bhd.

First Edition July 2011
2nd Print December 2019

The author's moral rights have been asserted. All rights reserved worldwide. No part of this book may be copied, used, subsumed, or exploited in fact, field of thought or general idea, by any other authors or persons, or be stored in a retrieval system, transmitted or reproduced in any way, including but not limited to digital copying and printing in any form whatsoever worldwide without the prior agreement and written permission of the publisher.

Quantity discounts of JY Books titles are available for educational, business or sales promotional use. For information, please contact:

JY Books Sdn. Bhd. (659134-T)
19-3, The Boulevard, Mid Valley City, 59200 Kuala Lumpur, Malaysia.
Tel : +603-2284 8080 | Fax : +603-2284 1218 | Email : info@jy-books.com

DISCLAIMER:

The publisher JY Books Sdn Bhd and the author, Hung Hin Cheong, have made their best efforts to produce this high quality, informative and helpful book. They have verified the technical accuracy of the information and contents of this book. Any information pertaining to the events, occurrences, dates and other details relating to the person or persons, dead or alive, and to the companies have been verified to the best of their abilities based on information obtained or extracted from various websites, newspaper clippings and other public media. However, they make no representation or warranties of any kind with regard to the contents of this book and accept no liability of any kind for any losses or damages caused or alleged to be caused directly or indirectly from using the information contained herein.

Table of Contents

Foreword by Joey Yap		iv
Introduction		vi
There're Stars and Stars and Stars…		xi
Chapter 1:	Dynamic & Static	1
Chapter 2:	Husband & Wife & the Kids	13
Chapter 3:	Some Conjunctions, Good & Bad	27
Chapter 4:	Of Growth & Control	37
Chapter 5:	Man & Woman	45
Chapter 6:	Ushering in Wealth	57
Chapter 7:	To Redeem a Clash	63
Chapter 8:	More of Growth & Control	71
Chapter 9:	Physical & Emotional Distress	87
Chapter 10:	More the Merrier	97
Chapter 11:	Health Issues	101
Chapter 12:	Of Minors & Seniors	109
Chapter 13:	Landform Issues	115
Chapter 14:	More Conjunctions, Good & Bad	121
Chapter 15:	Incapacitated, Out of Place	131
Chapter 16:	Special P5 Charts	137
Chapter 17:	Double Sitting, Double Facing	143
Chapter 18:	Rich & Famous	149
Chapter 19:	Any Facing, Crossing the Line	155
Chapter 20:	Recalcitrant Stars	161
Chapter 21:	4-Graveyards, 4-Growths	165
Chapter 22:	In Closing…	171
Appendix-1	The Story of "Inverse Siren, Hidden Siren (反吟伏吟)"	175
Appendix-2	"Castle Gate Formula (城門訣)"	191
Appendix-3	Star Conjunctions – A Bird's Eye View	205
Bibliography		212
About the Author		213

Foreword
By Joey Yap

In his new book, **Secrets of Xuan Kong**, Hung Hin Cheong takes a look at forms and star combinations, the basis of Xuan Kong Feng Shui. The book lays a solid foundation for further study of secret Xuan Kong techniques, especially those used in the Xuan Kong Feng Shui system.

Never before has anyone attempted to translate the texts featured and commentated them in English, meaning that Mr Hung has covered brand new ground in this indispensable book.

Mr Hung is a successful businessman and full-time property investor, a busy man who still managed to find time to do his own research and write this book. It is truly a labour of love. I can say, having read and studied Xuan Kong for many years, that his work here is truly remarkable.

Secrets of Xuan Kong is a translation based on the classic texts by the legendary Song Dynasty Feng Shui master, *Wu Jing Luan* 吳景鸞. Well-known Xuan Kong methods, its terminology and famous 'secret' techniques like Castle Gate Formula 城門訣, Fan Yin 反吟 and Fu Yin 伏吟 owe their roots to this classic. It is referenced by many famous Qing Dynasty (1644-1911) masters like *Shen Zhu Reng* 沈竹礽, and late Qing Dynasty/early Republic masters like *Tan Yang Wu* 談養吾 and *Kong Zhao Su* 孔昭蘇.

For the first time, Mr Hung has painstakingly translated the ancient texts into English for the modern audience, complementing his work with insightful commentaries and anecdotes. This book is invaluable for any serious Feng Shui practitioner and student, enabling them to take their studies to the next level and expand their understanding.

I suggest re-reading this book often as you progress in your study. The more you read it, the more profound your understanding will be. Reading this book once isn't enough. Read and reread. I promise you, you will make discoveries every time you read through it and as you learn more elsewhere, you can periodically revisit it and pick up more still. This book is a resource that keeps on giving!

On a personal note, I wish a book like this existed when I was studying Feng Shui twenty years ago. Students these days can count themselves lucky to have Mr Hung provide them with this invaluable reference.

Mr Hung continues to impress me with his relentless enthusiasm, diligence and contributions to the Xuan Kong Feng Shui field. I hope that this book will inspire and motivate you in your own studies on the subject.

Warm regards,
Joey Yap

Joey Yap
Founder of Mastery Academy of Chinese Metaphysics
July 2011

www.joeyyap.com
www.facebook.com/joeyyapFB

Introduction

There are 4 classics widely held to be the cornerstones of *xuan kong* Flying Stars *fengshui*. They are:

- Secrets of *xuan kong*   玄空秘旨
- Ode to Mysticism   玄機賦
- Ode to Flying Stars   飛星賦
- Purple White Script   紫白訣

"Secrets of *xuan kong*" was written by Wu Jing Luan (吳景鸞, circa 1040), a legendary Song Dynasty *fengshui* master. After Wu's death, the book disappeared for some 500 years, reportedly hidden in a cave where Wu used to meditate, until its accidental discovery by a Ming Dynasty *fengshui* scholar named Xu Shan Ji (徐善繼, circa 1580). Since then, the book was held in awe as a priceless treasure, and its circulation restricted to a close circle of *xuan kong* masters. However, that did not prevent the appearance of several slightly different versions - probably the outcome of iterative hand-copying or oral recitation.

It was not until 1836 that the renowned *xuan kong* master Zhang Zhong Shan (章仲山) included a version of "Secrets", together with his annotations thereof, in his treatise "Important Pointers to the Heart's Eye (心眼指要)". By then, the original text already came with 2 sets of annotations: an "Original Annotation (原註)" of uncertain authorship; and "Bao's Annotation (鮑註)" attributed to Bao Shi Xuan (鮑士選), of whom very little is known.

Even in Zhang's time, the dissemination of *xuan kong* knowledge was strictly controlled, and few people outside his closed-door "Wu Chang Lineage (無常派)" had any access to it.

The first master who taught *xuan kong* openly was Shen Zhu Reng (沈竹礽, 1849~1906). "Secrets" and the other 3 *xuan kong* classics were discussed in his classes, but Shen did not publish any of his writings. It was left to his son Shen Zu Mian (沈祖綿), and contemporaries, to edit and compile the elder Shen's class notes into a book called "Shen's *xuan kong* Studies (沈氏玄空學)", first published in 1925.

In Shen's book, "Secrets" was presented with 3 sets of annotations: "Original Annotation"; "Bao's Annotation"; and "Zhang's Annotation".

Shen's rendition of "Secrets" differed from Zhang's, but not materially. As Shen's book quickly became the de-facto standard text for *xuan kong* studies, Shen's version became more popular, and in this book it is referred to as the "popular version". Where there are differences between the popular version and Zhang's, the latter is also stated for comparison.

The author Wu Jing Luan was clearly an accomplished scholar keen to demonstrate his literary skills. The book was written in the style of matching couplets throughout, liberally embellished with idioms, metaphors and allusions. Whilst these literary devices made beautiful poetry, they did so at the expense of clarity and precision.

Of course this malady is not exclusive to "Secrets". Many classical *fengshui* texts are similarly infected. If the ancient masters were so intent on concealing information, I wonder why they bothered to write at all. One explanation often ventured is that it was necessary to protect such wondrous secrets from unscrupulous people, but what good would that serve if the information fell into virtuous hands who then messed up the interpretation?

"Secrets" attracted commentaries from many *fengshui* scholars past and present, but all in Chinese. One only has to search for the words "玄空秘旨" in the Internet to guage the book's popularity. The cacophony of divergent interpretations attests to the ambiguity of the original text and the confusion it has created.

From my research, which was by no means exhaustive, the following writers stood out as being original thinkers: Shen Zu Mian (沈祖綿), Kong Zhao Su (孔昭蘇), Zhong Yi Ming (鐘義明) and Ke Jian Cheng (柯建成), but that doesn't mean I'd agree with them all the time. Some other writers merely echoed other people's work without contributing any original idea. I trust my readers will not relegate this book and its author to that heap ☺

A special mention must be made of the book "Secrets of *xuan kong* - Refined Explanations (玄空秘旨精解)" by the contemporary writer Zhang Jue Ming (張覺明). The book compiled the annotations of several writers past and present. That simplified cross-referencing considerably.

Secrets of Xuan Kong

Now what makes "Secrets" so worthy of our attention?

Firstly, despite its quirkiness, the book makes a good text book for learning advanced *xuan kong* Flying Stars. Once the student gets past plotting the chart and looking for the "best" Stars to locate the door and the bed, "Secrets" steps in to look at the Stars as dynamic and static entities. The text focuses on the Stars' interactions between themselves and with the external landforms, as these interactions form the very basis of *xuan kong* Flying Stars.

The discussions are intellectual and yet practical. No single book can be expected to cover everything there is to know about *xuan kong*, but "Secrets" has done a better job than most. One could conceivably conduct a creditable Flying Stars *fengshui* audit going by "Secrets" alone, without recourse to other sources.

Secondly, "Secrets" holds an impressive repertoire of Star conjunctions and their effects, enough to enable a *xuan kong* practitioner to make predictions in a variety of situations.

The conjunctions listed are not exhaustive. More importantly, the text demonstrates by way of examples how Star conjunctions may be read. It is perfectly in order for practitioners to interpret Star conjunctions on the fly, as long as the deductions are logically derived.

In fact *xuan kong* Flying Stars is less of a tool for building layout design than a means to predict events that are likely to befall the occupants of a property, given the property's location and the timing. Some call it "divination", but I'm not sure divine intervention is called for. As they say, "it's all written in the Stars". One only has to learn how to interpret the signs.

"Secrets" and the other 3 "cornerstones" of *xuan kong* are the chief protagonists of *xuan kong* as a predictive technique. To make predictions using *xuan kong* is a skill that can be learned and then honed to astonishing accuracy through practice. Nothing spiritual about it, but to the uninitiated, it looks almost like divine revelation.

This book is intended for students who already have some basic knowledge of *xuan kong* Flying Stars. It is assumed they know how to plot a chart and are comfortable with terms like "forward flight", "reverse flight", "Prosperous Sitting Prosperous Facing (旺山旺水)", "Up Mountain Down Water (上山下水)", "Double Sitting (雙星到坐)", "Double Facing (雙星到向)", "Direct/Indirect Spirit (零神正神)"; and also with the concept of a Star's timeliness. These students will surely be able to benefit from this book. It will take them to a much higher level of competence as *xuan kong* practitioners.

This book is never intended to be light reading material. Sing and dance it will not, but to relieve the dryness, I have tagged on sidebars here and there that relate some interesting anecdotes gleaned from my background research. These snippets provide a glimpse of Chinese culture and traditions against which "Secrets" was written.

There is certainly no shortage of published material on "Secrets" in the Chinese language, but to the best of my knowledge, no one has yet translated it into English, let alone commented on the text line by line.

Like other old Chinese texts, there were originally no paragraphs or punctuation marks. These were added later to improve readability. The demarcation into chapters is quite arbitrary, and the line numbers are added for easy reference only. The chapter headings are figments of my imagination and have little bearing on the content.

At the end of each chapter, the topics covered are summarized in point form, to provide quick references. In addition, all the Star conjunctions are collated and tabulated in Appendix-3, in an orderly manner, and listing both positives and negatives for a balanced view.

2 popular *xuan kong* topics called "Inverse Siren, Hidden Siren (反吟伏吟)" and "Castle Gate Formula (城門訣)" are discussed in Appendices 1 and 2. One is unlikely to find a more meticulous explanation of these topics anywhere else, in English or in Chinese.

Even allowing for the idiosyncrasies of ancient classics, "Secrets" has proven to be an unusually difficult document to decipher. Were it not for the broad spectrum of *fengshui* material published in Taiwan, and the wealth of information readily accessible on the Internet, I could not possibly have completed the task. At times the going was indeed tough, but the thought of being the first to bring this ancient masterpiece to the English speaking *fengshui* community saw me through.

Only the most egotistic and foolhardy of writers will dare claim that his interpretation of "Secrets" is perfect. There are bound to be shortcomings, but I am confident this humble effort of mine has made the grade, or in Master Wu Jing Luan's language, it has not "fallen outside of Sun Shan" (idiom explained in Line SX70).

I am indebted to Master Joey Yap for gracing this book with his Foreword. Master Joey is a gifted teacher and prolific writer of Chinese Metaphysics in English. His invaluable contribution to the English speaking world of CM is an inspiration to the rest of us. May this book add just one more candle to help light up the wonders of CM that have hidden in the shadows of human awareness for so long.

from the ramblings of one hhc, a fengshui crazee
December 2010

There're Stars and Stars and Stars…

"Secrets of *xuan kong* (玄空秘旨)" is all about the Purple White Stars #1 to #9. In trying to explain the lines of the poem, I have approached the lines from the angle of modern *xuan kong* Flying Stars, as for example, the Sitting Star (坐星) and Facing Star (向星) are given prominence in much of the discussions.

However, the modern *xuan kong* Flying Stars system was first taught by Shen Zhu Reng (沈竹礽) only in the late 19th/early 20th Century, whereas "Secrets" was written about 900 years before Shen. We are not even sure Sitting Star and Facing Star, as we know them today, existed back then. In all likelihood, the author Wu Jing Luan (吳景鸞) had other Stars in mind, typically the *luo shu* Stars, Period Stars, Annual Stars, landform Stars, etc.

The commentaries, both mine and other writers', are written in the language of modern Flying Stars, also called Shen's Flying Stars, simply because that is the version best known to modern practitioners and students. But it is by no means the only version. Students are cautioned against being conditioned into thinking that Flying Stars necessarily have to do with Sitting Star and Facing Star. A broader mind-set is needed.

That brings to mind the predicament many students faced when they are confronted with irregularly shaped buildings, or buildings of uncertain age. How should they go about establishing the facing, or the Period, of such a building? And without this information, how is it possible to draw up the Flying Stars chart?

The answer is: don't be dogmatic. We do not have to draw up the chart every time.

The *luo shu* Stars, current Period Stars, Annual Stars and landform Stars are often enough for us to perform a credible *fengshui* audit. "Secrets" provides us with a means to do that.

Chapter 1
Dynamic & Static

CHAPTER 1:
Dynamic & Static

SX01: 不知來路，焉知入路，盤中八卦皆空。

Not knowing the approach road, how does one know the incoming road? The 8 Trigrams in the *luo pan* all become void.

[章作：不知變易，但知不易，九星八卦皆空。

Zhang's version: Not knowing the dynamic entities and knowing only the static, the 9 stars and the 8 Trigrams all become void.]

"Approach road (來路)" refers to dynamic entities, i.e. those that change with time, and in particular the distribution of the Period Stars in the 9-grid space that changes every 20 years.

In Period-1, Star-1 enters the central palace; Star-2 goes to the *qian* (NW) palace; Star-3 goes to *dui* (W) palace; and so on in forward progression along the *luo shu* path (Fig-1a). When Period-2 arrives, the Period Stars shift locations: Star-2 moves into the centre; Star-3 goes to *qian*; Star-4 to *dui*; and so on (Fig-1b). It is currently Period-8 (2004 - 2023CE) (Fig-1c). This is the very essence of *xuan kong* Flying Stars.

In *xuan kong* jargon, this distribution of the Stars is called the "Period Plate (運盤)" or "Heaven Plate (天盤)".

"Incoming road (入路)" refers to the static entities, i.e. those that remain constant at all times. One manifestation of that is the *luo shu* numbers in the 9-grid space (Fig-1d), with Star-5 at the centre; Star-6 at *qian*; Star-7 at *dui*; etc. This star distribution does not change with time. In *xuan kong* jargon, it is called the "Starting Plate (元旦盤)" or "Earth Plate (地盤)".

At this juncture, it should be explained that word "Plate (盤)" in *xuan kong* has a different meaning from the word "Plate (盤)" used to describe the concentric rings of the *luo pan*. Same word, different meanings. In *xuan kong*, a particular distribution of the Stars 1 to 9 in a 9-grid space is called a "Plate". We have already seen "Period Plate" and "Starting Plate". Soon we will be seeing other "Plates" such as "Sitting Plate (山盤)", "Facing Plate (向盤)", etc. [However, we shall not be explaining how the "Sitting Plate" and "Facing Plate" are derived. For this, please refer to entry level books on Flying Stars.]

Chapter 1: Dynamic & Static

9	5	7
8	1	3
4	6	2

Fig-1a: Period-1 "Period Plate"

1	6	8
9	2	4
5	7	3

Fig-1b: Period-2 "Period Plate"

7	3	5
6	8	1
2	4	9

Fig-1c: Period-8 "Period Plate"

❹	❾	❷
❸	❺	❼
❽	❶	❻

Fig-1d: "Starting Plate"

Fig-1: "Period Plates" & "Starting Plate"

The Later Heaven arrangement of the 8 Trigrams (*qian* at NW; *dui* at W; etc.) also does not change with time, and is therefore a static entity.

Another static entity is the distribution of the 24 Mountains on the *luo pan*. [*xuan kong* uses the *san yuan luo pan* which has only one 24-Mountains ring. Note that the *yin/yang* polarities on this ring differ from the *san he luo pan*.]

In *xuan kong* terminology, landforms such as mountains, water mouths, large buildings, road junctions, etc. are often called "Stars". By and large, these physical Stars do not change with time, and are therefore another manifestation of static entities. [Having said that, it's not at all unusual to have mountains flattened and rivers diverted these days, but I guess the old *xuan kong* masters couldn't imagine that.]

Line SX01 simply states that to assess the *fengshui* of a property, it is not enough to consider only the static entities. It is also necessary to take into account dynamic entities that in *xuan kong* are represented by the Stars 1 to 9. Failure to do so could nullify an assessment, hence the word "void".

[In this very first line of the text, 2 rather strange terms were used: "approach road" and "incoming road". Almost every writer who commented on the text interpreted the terms to mean dynamic and static entities, but nobody bothered to explain why. Such is the cloak of mystery wrapped around ancient classics – how infuriating! ☹]

Chapter 1: Dynamic & Static

> **SX02:** 未識內堂，焉識外堂，局裡五行盡錯。
>
> Before recognizing the internal hall, how does one recognize the external hall? The 5 elements of the structure will be all wrong.
>
> [章作：不識三般，那識兩片，凡屬五行盡錯。
>
> Zhang's version: Not recognizing the "3 kinds", how does one recognize the "2 slices"? The 5 elements to which they belong will be all wrong.]

"Internal hall (內堂)" refers to the prosperous Period Star and the Flying Stars distribution that arises from it. The Stars are normally written inside a 9-grid space, hence "internal".

"External hall (外堂)" refers to the landforms outside, hence "external".

In other words, if the facing of a property is selected based on external landforms only, and the timeliness of the Flying Stars is ignored, then the 5 elements of the "structure" will be incorrect.

In *fengshui* parlance, the word "structure" is loosely defined, and often ambiguous [sometimes on purpose, I think]. In the present context, "structure" describes the 9 palaces of the chart. In other words, the elements (Metal, Wood, Water, Fire and Earth) associated with each palace are not constant. They depend on the Stars resident at the palace in any one Period.

Master Zhang Zhong Shan's (章仲山) version employs 2 jargon terms "3 kinds" and "2 slices", which are in fact fairly common *xuan kong* expressions.

"3 kinds (三般)" simply means 3 different groupings of Stars. The term is applied to different groupings in various *fengshui* texts, but in the present context, "3 kinds" is an abbreviation of the expression "3 kinds of *gua* (三般卦)", referring to the 3 sub-sectors, or "Mountains", under each Trigram on the *luo pan*. In the *san yuan luo pan*, the 24-Mountains are divided into 3 groups, as follows:

- *zi, wu, mao, you, qian, kun, gen, xun* (子午卯酉乾坤艮巽) belong to the group called "Heavenly Dragons (天元龍)";

Chapter 1: Dynamic & Static

- *chen, xu, chou, wei, jia, geng, bing, ren* (辰戌丑未甲庚丙壬) belong to the group called "Earthly Dragons (地元龍)";

- *yin, shen, si, hai, yi, xin, ding, gui* (寅申巳亥乙辛丁癸) belong to the group called "Human Dragons (人元龍)".

[I've always found the rampant use of the word "Dragon" disconcerting, but I guess we'll have to put up with the ancient masters' inclination to dramatize and mystify.]

Within each group, some of the Mountains (Dragons) are of the *yang* polarity whilst others are *yin*.

The term "2 slices (兩片)" comes from the line in the classic "Green Satchel Preface (青囊序)" that says "The Dragons are divided into 2 slices to become *yin* and *yang* (龍分兩片陰陽取)".

Taking the 2 parts together, Master Zhang simply said that one must understand the Periodic changes at the 24-Mountains before one could tell whether the Mountain's current polarity is *yin* or *yang*.

Still mystified? Okay, let's go back to the core of *xuan kong* Flying Stars. Fig-2a shows the 24-Mountains Plate of the *san yuan luo pan* with the *luo shu* Stars 1-9 inserted for convenience. The Mountains with clear characters on dark background are *yang*, and the ones with dark characters on clear are *yin*. This distribution of the Mountains and Stars is a static entity.

Chapter 1: Dynamic & Static

Fig-2b shows a similar distribution for Period-8 when Star-8 flies into the centre.

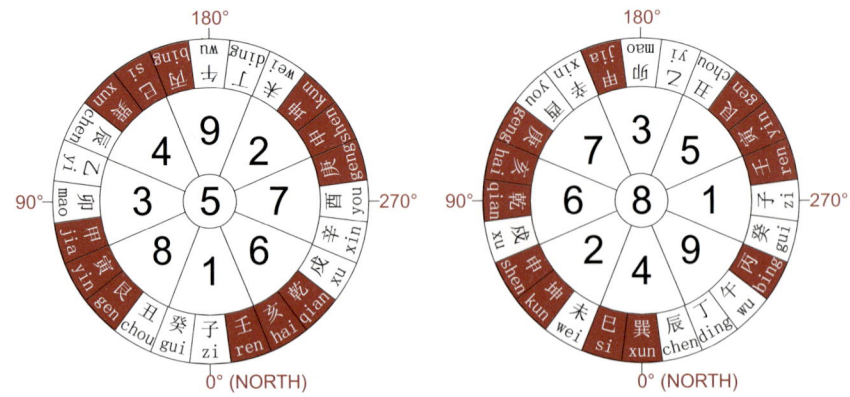

Fig-2a: static 24-Mountains   Fig-2b: Period-8 24-Mountains

Fig-2: polarity changes

Comparing the 2 charts, can you now see that what was *ren* (壬) in Fig-2a has now become *chen* (辰) in Fig-2b? Whereas *ren* was originally *yang*, the same Mountain has become *yin* in Period-8! Note that this change of polarity does not occur at every Mountain. For instance, what was originally *chou* (丑) has now become *wei* (未), but both are *yin*.

This is what Master Zhang was driving at. The polarity of any location changes with time, and hence requires different treatments at different times. This is the specialty of *xuan kong*.

The use of jargon notwithstanding, Master Zhang's version of Line SX02 is, in my opinion, much more elegant, compared with arbitrary terms like "internal hall" and "external hall".

Reading between the lines, Lines SX01 and SX02 contain a hidden jibe at *san he fengshui*. *san he* relies primarily on landform features to establish facings, and landforms are generally static. The *xuan kong* practitioners are implying that *san he* techniques are ineffective because they do not take into account changing times. For some reason, *xuan kong* practitioners were [some still are] fond of belittling other *fengshui* schools to elevate their own standing. [Could this irritating and completely unnecessary behavior be driven by inferiority complex?]

Chapter 1: Dynamic & Static

> **SX03:** 乘氣脫氣，轉禍福於指掌之間。
>
> Being able to ride or discard the *qi*, the power to turn misfortune to good fortune lies in one's palm.
>
> [章作：顛之倒之，轉禍福於指掌之間。
>
> Zhang's version: Toppling it and turning it over, the power to turn misfortune to good fortune lies in one's palm.]

The expression "ride the *qi*" comes from the line in the Burial Book (葬書) that says "To bury is to ride on *sheng qi* (葬者乘生氣也)". In the *xuan kong* context, to ride the *qi* means to make use of the current and forthcoming prosperous Stars. In Period-8, that would mean Star-8, Star-9, and Star-1.

To "discard the *qi*" is simply the reverse of that, i.e. making use of expired *qi*. That would mean Star-7, Star-6, and the Stars further behind.

Line SX03 says that if one is able to use the Stars correctly, then one should be able to pursue the good fortune and avert the bad. The reference to the palm also alludes to the traditional way a practitioner tracks the movement of the Stars using his fingers.

In Master Zhang's version, the expression "toppling it and turning it over" is a throwback to the line in the classic "Green Satchel Oracles (青囊奧語)" that says "toppling over this way and that, jewels are to be found in each of the 24-Mountains (顛顛倒，二十四山有珠寶)".

"Toppling and turning" refers to the forward and reverse flights of the Stars along the *luo shu* path. In certain instances (when a particular Mountain on the "Period Plate" is of *yang* polarity) a Star flies forward, for example, Star-8 at the centre; Star-9 goes to *qian*; Star-1 to *dui*; and so on. At other times the same Star flies in reverse, i.e. Star-8 at the centre; Star-7 goes to *qian*; Star-6 to *dui*; and so on. Knowing how to fly the Stars means knowing where one could find and use the prosperous Stars.

Hence both the popular version and Master Zhang's are really saying the same thing.

Chapter 1: Dynamic & Static

> **SX04:** 左挨右挨，辨吉凶於毫芒之際。
>
> Leaning left and leaning right, to tell apart good fortune from bad down to the minutest detail.

Lines SX03 and SX04 make up a couplet (2-line poem), where the second line serves as a response to the first line following certain strict rhythmic rules. Very often the second line merely echoes the first, and this appears to be one of those cases.

"Leaning left" means flying the Stars in reverse, and "leaning right" means flying them forward.

The bit about "… down to the minutest detail" is, in my view, more figurative than factual. Bragging rights I guess…

To expand on the expression "leaning left and leaning right", it is appropriate to mention herein one of the basic skills of Flying Stars analysis. When a Star at the centre, be it Sitting Star or Facing Star, flies in reverse, the prosperous Star of the Period will invariably land at the relevant palace, i.e. when the Sitting Star flies in reverse, the prosperous Star will land at the Sitting palace; and when the Facing Star flies in reverse, the prosperous Star will land at the Facing palace. Conversely, if the flight is forward, then the prosperous Star will land at the palace diametrically opposite.

As such, with one look at the Stars in the central palace a skilled practitioner should be able to identify the structure of the chart: whether "Prosperous Facing Prosperous Sitting (旺山旺向)", or "Up Mountain Down Water (上山下水)", or "Double Facing (雙星到向)", or "Double Sitting (雙星到坐)", without having to plot out the whole chart.

A "Double Facing" chart can also be described as "Prosperous Facing but Down Water"; and a "Double Sitting" chart as "Prosperous Sitting but Up Mountain".

Chapter 1: Dynamic & Static

> **SX05:** 一天星斗，運用只在中央。
>
> Of all the stars in the heavens, use only those at the centre.
>
> **SX06:** 千瓣蓮花，根蒂生於點滴。
>
> The lotus has a thousand petals, but its roots and stalk grow from a tiny drop (of water).
>
> [章作：九曜干支，旋轉由乎北極。
>
> Zhang's version: The 9 Stars and the Stems and Branches revolve around the North Pole.]

Lines SX05 and SX06 are again 2 parts of a couplet. It is best to read them together.

The first line describes the multiple Stars that inhabit a typical Flying Stars chart. It says the key Stars are found at the central palace. Everything else is derived from those.

In the popular version, Line SX06 invokes the imagery of a lotus flower. It makes an elegant rhythmic response to the earlier line.

Master Zhang's version has more substance in it. "9 Stars and the Stems and Branches" describes the Flying Stars 1 to 9 and the *luo pan*'s 24-Mountains that are associated with each of the Stars. For example, Star-1 with *ren/zi/gui* (壬/子/癸); Star-2 with *wei/kun/shen* (未/坤/申); and so on.

The line says all the Stars and the Mountains will change when there is a change at the centre, except that it is said in a rather roundabout way. The ancient astronomers observed that all the visible stars seemed to revolve around a fixed point in the Northern skies. Modern astronomy calls this point the "Celestial North Pole". The ancient Chinese astronomers called it the "Emperor Star".
[See panel below for a brief discussion on ancient Chinese astronomy.]

It would appear to an observer on earth that the whole sky revolves around this star at the Celestial North Pole, much like the disk of a *luo pan* revolving around its pivot at the "Heaven Pool (天池)". In other words, the Celestial North Pole is seen to be the centre of the universe.

In making reference to the North Pole, Master Zhang was obviously trying to tie the second line back to the first line which talked about the heavenly stars.

Chapter 1: Dynamic & Static

The age-old concept of "Celestial Sphere", though not factual, still serves as a useful model in modern astronomy. In this model, all the heavenly bodies as seen from the earth are imagined to be stuck on the surface of an imaginary sphere. In other words, actual distances are ignored. The earth is placed at the centre of the sphere.

The ancient Chinese astronomers worked on a very similar model of the universe. They observed that all the stars appeared to revolve around one of the stars in the "Covert Purple Enclosure (紫微垣)" in the Northern skies. They called this star the "Emperor Star (帝星)". In modern language, that would be "North Polar Star".

The Chinese astronomers further postulated that this "Emperor Star", acting through its neighbour, the "Crown Prince Star (太子星)", ruled the universe, and these universal laws affected all human endeavours on earth.

All students of Metaphysics would have come across the "North Dipper (北斗星)" Asterism. The "Dipper" was thought to be the royal carriage that circumnavigated the "Covert Purple Enclosure" to disseminate the royal commands to the rest of the universe. For example, the direction to which the handle of the "Dipper" pointed heralded the coming of the 4 Seasons on earth.

The modern astronomical name of "Emperor Star" is Beta Ursae Minoris (symbol βUMi) and its classical Greek name is Kochab. The modern name of "Crown Prince Star" is Gama Ursae Minoris (symbol γUMi), Greek name Pherkad.

With our modern understanding of the astronomical phenomenon known as Precession, it is calculated that in the period 1500BCE - 500CE, Kochab and Pherkad were indeed the twin North Polar Stars. This was the time when the ancient Chinese astronomers studied and mapped the stars. So their observations proved remarkably accurate. Not bad, especially as it was all done with the naked eye.

Since that time, Precession has caused the Polar Star to shift. The current North Polar Star is Alfa Ursae Minoris (αUMi), more commonly known as Polaris. By 3000CE it will shift again.

The first 6 lines of the text serve as a primer, emphasizing the importance of changing the Star distribution from Period to Period, i.e. every 20 years. From this point on, the text turns to individual Stars and Star conjunctions, and the prognoses that could be drawn from them. We are now diving into the core of the text.

Chapter 1 – Summary

➢ The energy pattern of the universe changes continuously, and *xuan kong* represents this by 9 virtual entities trading places periodically in 9 boxes arranged in a 3x3 matrix. The entities are called "Stars" numbered from 1 to 9, and the boxes make up our familiar 9-grid space.

➢ The continuum of time is divided into 9 "Periods", each of 20 years duration. In different Periods, different Stars will reside in the 9 boxes, called "palaces". As the Stars change with time, they are dynamic entities.

➢ Environmental features like mountains and water, called "landforms", exert a major impact on the energy pattern, called "*qi* distribution", of the area. As mountains and water do not usually change over time, relatively speaking, they are static entities.

➢ Chapter 1 goes to great lengths to stress that to assess the *fengshui* potential of a property, both the dynamic Stars and the static landforms must be evaluated together. Failing that, the conclusions drawn will be incorrect.

Chapter 2
Husband & Wife & the Kids

CHAPTER 2:
Husband & Wife & the Kids

SX07: 夫婦相逢於道路，卻嫌阻隔不通情。

Husband and wife meet on the road, but complain of impediments to their mutual affection.

The text is fond of using allegories (talking in riddles).

In this instance, "husband" refers to the prosperous Star of the current Period on the "Facing Plate", and "wife" refers to the prosperous Star on the "Sitting Plate". In Period-8, for example, Star-8 of the "Facing Plate" becomes the "husband", and Star-8 of the "Sitting Plate" becomes the "wife".

[The Chinese term "山盤" may be translated as "Mountain Plate" or "Sitting Plate", just as the term "山星" may be translated as "Mountain Star" or "Sitting Star". Then again, a physical mountain is sometimes also called a "Mountain Star". To avoid possible confusion, we shall always use the terms "Sitting Plate" and "Sitting Star" in this book when we are talking about the virtual Stars.]

xuan kong theory requires that the "husband" sees water (or at least low ground or open space). The "wife" on the other hand should see a mountain (or at least high ground or a dense environment). In addition, the said water and mountain must be of good quality. [A good mountain is one that is wholesome and not jagged or deformed; and water is good if it is clear and flows gently.] If those conditions are fulfilled in a given chart, the chart is said to be supported by the physical landforms. In the words of Line SX07, the "husband" and "wife" are able to enjoy mutual affection.

Conversely, if the required conditions are not met, as for example if the "husband" sees a mountain and the "wife" sees water; or if the mountain and water, though in the right locations, are of poor quality, then the chart cannot be considered good as it lacks the support of the landforms. In such a case, the "husband" and "wife" are said to suffer from impediments to their mutual affection.

Chapter 2: Husband & Wife & the Kids

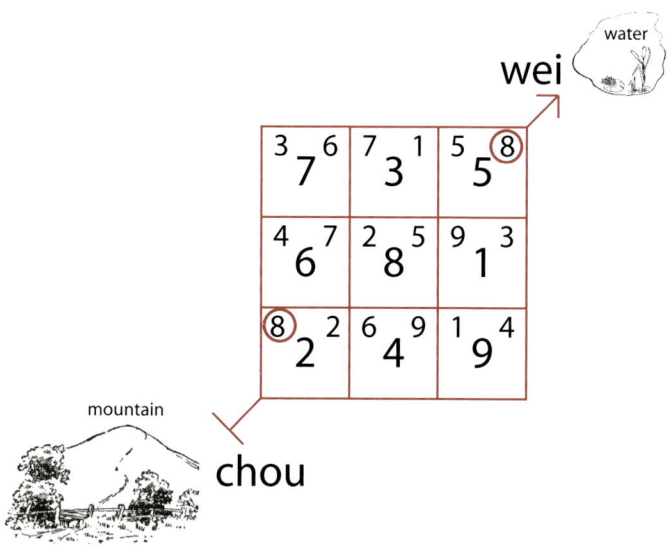

Fig-3: chart supported by landforms

Fig-3 is the chart of a Period-8 *chou* sitting *wei* facing (丑山未向) property. In this chart, Star-8 of the "Facing Plate" is located at the Facing palace, and Star-8 of the "Sitting Plate" is located at the Sitting Palace. By definition, this is a "Prosperous Sitting Prosperous Facing (旺山旺向)" chart, which holds great potential.

Line SX07 reminds us that for the chart to work, it must be supported by water (or low ground or open space) at the front of the property, and a physical mountain (or high ground or dense environment) at the rear. If these conditions are not met, the chart will not deliver the desired results.

Flying Stars practitioners often err by reading too much into the numbers on a chart and paying scant attention to landforms. The classics have made it quite clear that Flying Stars are only meaningful if they are corroborated by physical landforms. Regrettably, this precondition is sometimes overlooked in one's eagerness to decipher a chart.

By extension of the argument presented herein, an "Up Mountain Down Water (上山下水)" chart may not be that bad, provided it has the support of the physical landforms. In other words, if a property sees high ground in front and water at the rear, then an "Up Mountain Down Water" chart could be preferred over a "Prosperous Sitting Prosperous Facing" chart.

Secrets of Xuan Kong

Chapter 2: Husband & Wife & the Kids

It must be stated that the above interpretation of Line SX07 is not the only one, but it is the interpretation preferred by modern writers. In Master Zhang's annotation of the original text, he ventured a different interpretation. For completeness, I should mention his interpretation here, even though it could create confusion.

To Zhang, "husband and wife meet..." refers to the Stars at which physical water and physical mountains are found relative to a given property. He further wrote that the *yin/yang* of the mountain and water Stars should be complementary. [Note: mountain and water Stars are not synonymous with Sitting and Facing Stars in this context.] In other words, if the mountain is located at a *yin* Star, the water should be located at a *yang* Star, or vice versa. In this way, "husband" and "wife" are said to have met and are able to express their mutual affection.

The confusion lies in Zhang's use of the words *yin* and *yang* in this context. *yin* Stars and *yang* Stars? What did Zhang mean by that?

Subsequent writers have clarified that *yin* and *yang* as used by Zhang referred not to polarity but to the timeliness of the Stars. A Star in its active state, i.e. timely, is described as *yang*; whereas a Star in its passive state, i.e. out of timing, is described as *yin*. For example: in Period-7, Stars-7, 8 & 9 are *yang* and Stars-6, 5 & 4 are *yin*; whereas in Period-8, Stars 8, 9 & 1 are *yang* and Stars 7, 6 & 5 are *yin*.

According to Zhang, if the mountain is located at an untimely (*yin*) Star, and the water is also located at the same or another untimely (*yin*) Star, then "husband" and "wife" are said to be facing impediments to their mutual affection. Likewise a timely (*yang*) mountain and timely (*yang*) water conjunction is also detrimental.

[Clearly this interpretation arose from the following statement in the "Green Satchel Classic (青囊經)":

陰陽相見，福祿永貞；陰陽相乘，禍咎踵門。

yin and *yang* meeting, good fortune and wealth forever unwavering;
yin and *yang* riding, mishaps and ill fortune calling at the door.

The meeting of *yin* and *yang* is a prerequisite for the birth of all things in the universe.]

Regrettably Zhang did not clarify whether he was looking at the "Period Plate" for both mountain and water, or was it the "Sitting Plate" for mountain and "Facing Plate" for water. By omission, I would infer that he was referring to the "Period Plate" by itself.

Chapter 2: Husband & Wife & the Kids

Zhang did mention that even if the mountain and water are located at the right Stars, they are no good if the landforms are defective, meaning damaged mountain, gushing water, etc.

Whether or not one subscribes to Zhang's interpretation is unimportant. The key point is Zhang's assertion that Stars and landforms must be evaluated together. All later masters concurred on this point. Flying Stars on their own are impotent if they are not supported by the correct landforms.

Taking Zhang's interpretation one step further, one can surmise that the ideal locations for mountain and water should be the *he tu* combination Stars 1-6, 2-7, 3-8 and 4-9, as these are the natural "husband-and-wife" numbers. In other words, if the mountain is located at Star-1, then the ideal location for water will be Star-6, and so on. [Do not confuse this with the Direct/Indirect Spirit Rule (正神零神位). They are 2 different considerations.]

Chapter 2: Husband & Wife & the Kids

> **SX08:** 兒孫盡在於門庭，猶忌凶頑非孝義。
>
> The children and grandchildren are all gathered at the door, but the concern is they may be bad, stubborn and not filial.
>
> [章作：兒孫盡在於門庭，猶恐凶頑非孝義。
>
> Master Zhang used a different word, but the meaning is unaffected.]

If the current prosperous Star on the "Facing Plate" is the "husband" and the current prosperous Star on the "Sitting Plate" is the "wife", then the future prosperous Stars on both these Plates must represent the "children and grandchildren".

For example: in Period-8, Star-8 would represent the "husband" and "wife" on the "Facing Plate" and "Sitting Plate" respectively. Star-9 on both Plates would represent the "children"; and Star-1 the "grandchildren".

By an extension of the logic expounded in Line SX07, Star-9 and Star-1 on the "Facing Plate" should see water or lowland; and these same Stars on the "Sitting Plate" should see mountain or high ground. If this condition is fulfilled, the property's *fengshui* rating goes up several notches. In the language of Line SX08, the "children and grandchildren" are said to be of good character, obedient and filial. [Traditional Chinese culture requires kids to be all that, never mind if they are stupid or useless in everything else they do ☺]

Conversely, if mountains are found at the "children and grandchildren" Stars on the "Facing Plate"; or water is found at the same Stars on the "Sitting Plate"; or if the mountains and water are of inferior quality, then the "children and grandchildren" are said to be bad, stubborn and not filial. In other words, the property's *fengshui* is compromised even if the chart is otherwise excellent.

Chapter 2: Husband & Wife & the Kids

Some masters use these observations to make prognoses on the household's descendant luck. For example, if reverse bow water (convex side of a bow shaped river) cuts into a "children" or "grandchildren" Star on the "Facing Plate", the prediction could be that the household may be wealthy but the descendents will not be filial. Alternatively, if a deformed mountain is seen at a "children" or "grandchildren" Star on the "Sitting Plate", chances are the descendants could turn into thugs and criminals. Fig-4 illustrates such a scenario.

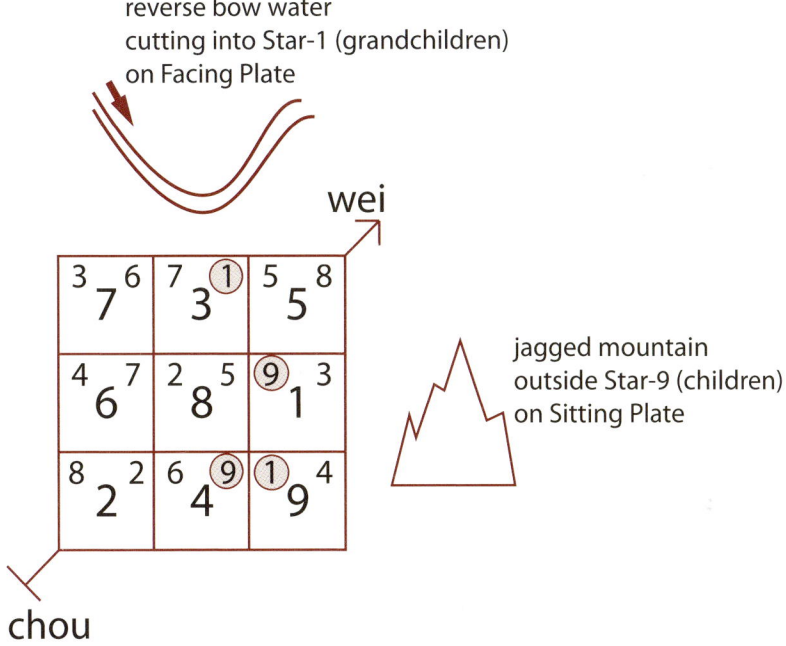

Fig-4: bad descendant luck

Chapter 2: Husband & Wife & the Kids

> **SX09:** 卦爻雜亂，異姓同居。
>
> If the lines of a Trigram are mixed up, different surnames will live under the same roof.

This line talks about landforms. If a landform straddles over 2 adjacent Mountains on the 24-Mountains Plate, it is said to have a mixed up Trigram. Another way of saying it is "crossing the line".

Each Trigram is subdivided into 3 Mountains on the *luo pan*: the ones at the centre (*zi*, *gen*, *mao*, *xun*, *wu*, *kun*, *you*, *qian*) are labeled "Heavenly Dragons (天元龍)"; the ones preceding them (*ren*, *chou*, *jia*, *chen*, *bing*, *wei*, *geng*, *xu*) are called "Earthly Dragons (地元龍)"; and the ones succeeding the "Heavenly Dragons" (*gui*, *yin*, *yi*, *si*, *ding*, *shen*, *xin*, *hai*) are called "Human Dragons (人元龍)".

Basically, a given landform such as an incoming mountain range or an incoming river should avoid crossing the line between 2 adjacent Mountains, i.e. the mountain range or meandering river should be contained within a single Mountain on the *luo pan*, for as far as the eye can see. The landform is then said to be "pure". For example, a landform that stays within *zi* or *gen* or *mao*, etc. is called a pure "Heavenly Dragon"; and a landform that confines itself to *ren*, *chou* or *jia*, etc. is called a pure "Earthly Dragon", and so on. Such "purity" is desired. If the landform crosses the line and straddles over 2 adjacent Mountains, it is no longer pure and is said to suffer from a "mixed up Trigram".

[How realistic is this penchant for "purity"? It's rare, to say the least. A landform like a mountain range (so-called "Incoming Dragon") will have to be exceedingly well behaved to stay within a single Mountain for as far as the eye can see. To sidestep the problem, *xuan kong* masters tend to ignore "Incoming Dragons" and focus instead on single mountains which they call "Stars".]

There are some auxiliary rules:

- A "Heavenly Dragon" landform is permitted to encroach into its adjacent "Human Dragon" but not into the "Earthly Dragon" on the other side;

- A "Human Dragon" landform is permitted to encroach into its adjacent "Heavenly Dragon" but not into the "Earthly Dragon" on the other side;

- An "Earthly Dragon" landform must remain pure. It must not encroach into either neighbour.

Chapter 2: Husband & Wife & the Kids

The logic is quite straightforward. A "Heavenly Dragon" and its adjacent "Human Dragon" are of the same polarity and they belong to the same Trigram on the *luo pan*. In the case of the "Earthly Dragon", its "Heavenly Dragon" neighbour is of the opposite polarity, and its "Human Dragon" neighbour on the other side belongs to another Trigram.

Simply put, it's ok if the 2 adjacent Mountains are of the same polarity and belong to the same Trigram. Otherwise, no.

The phrase "different surnames under the same roof" describes a woman's second marriage in which she brings along her children from a previous marriage – hence the different surnames. [And what's so wrong with that in today's society?]

Several old texts have listed a multitude of dire consequences for "crossing the line", including the death of one's spouse; no descendants; incest; debauchery; poverty; punishment at the hands of the law; etc. Believable? I'd take it with a pinch of salt. Old texts are prone to exaggerations. It is wise to evaluate their threats against actual observations.

Chapter 2: Husband & Wife & the Kids

> **SX10:** 吉凶相併，螟蛉爲嗣。
>
> If the beneficial merges with the harmful, the descendants will be "moth larvae" (metaphor for adopted children, see sidebar).

The line refers, rather obliquely, to the *xuan kong* concept of "Inverse/Hidden Sirens (反伏吟)". As the explanation of this concept is rather lengthy, I have relegated it to Appendix-1.

Briefly, a "Hidden Siren" occurs when the Sitting Star or Facing Star lands at a palace having the same *luo shu* Star, as for example Sitting or Facing Star-1 landing at *kan* palace; or when Sitting or Facing Star-8 lands at *gen* palace.

An "Inverse Siren" occurs when the Sitting or Facing Star lands at a palace at which the same *luo shu* Star resides at the palace diametrically opposite, as for example Sitting or Facing Star-1 landing at *li* palace.

[There are other types of "Inverse/Hidden Sirens". These are covered in Appendix-1.]

Such occurrences are viewed negatively, and the term "violating Inverse/Hidden Sirens" is coined to describe them. Old *xuan kong* texts threatened dire consequences for such violations, including life threatening situations and bankruptcies. Are they really so terrible? I wonder how much evidence has been gathered to support the unequivocal condemnations.

In any case, like other *xuan kong* taboos, an "Inverse/Hidden Siren" must be collaborated by negative landforms to unleash its belligerence. The worst offender in this instance is a crowded and oppressive environment, as in the case of a property hemmed in on all sides by sheer cliffs or densely packed buildings.

A "Siren" involving the Sitting Star will impact people luck; whereas a "Siren" involving the Facing Star will affect wealth.

A "Siren" at the Sitting palace is hard to resolve. Some old texts hinted at possible solutions but weren't very explicit. (See Appendix-1)

A "Siren" at the Facing palace may be resolved with water outside that palace.

"Sirens" at any of the other palaces are not as serious. An open space outside will effectively neutralize the threat. Moreover, the potential threat affects only those persons related to the afflicted Star. For example, a 2-2 "Siren" is potentially harmful to the mother of the household, or an old woman, or a Star-2 (*gua*-2) person, etc.

Chapter 2: Husband & Wife & the Kids

Fig-5 below cites some examples of "Hidden Siren".

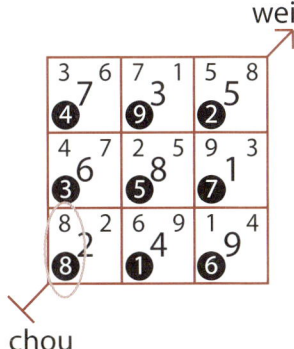

Fig-5a: HS @ Sitting palace

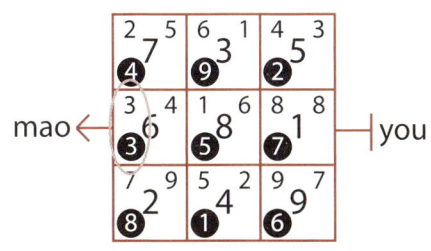

Fig-5b: HS @ Facing palace

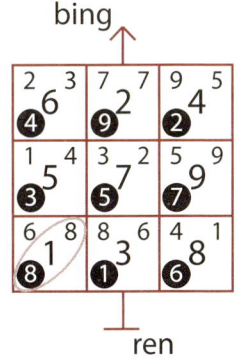

Fig-5c: HS @ other palaces

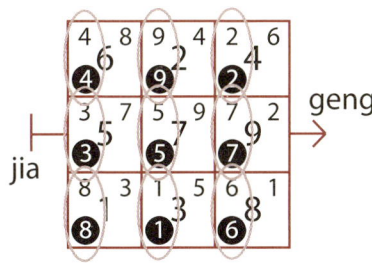

Fig-5d: HS all over

Fig-5: Hidden Sirens

Fig-5a: In Period-8, although a property sitting *chou* facing *wei* will have a "Prosperous Mountain Prosperous Water" chart, Sitting Star-8 also violates "Hidden Siren" (8-8) at the Sitting palace.

In Period-8, Star-8 is prosperous, and that effectively neutralizes the "Hidden Siren". The problem could arise come Period-9 when Star-8 loses its prosperous status. Strict (and paranoid) Flying Stars adherents may want to move out before 2024.

Chapter 2: Husband & Wife & the Kids

Fig-5b: A Period-8 property sitting *you* facing *mao* violates "Hidden Siren" (3-3) at the Facing palace. Having water or a roadway outside the Facing palace will resolve this problem.

If water is used, do check that it does not violate the "Direct/Indirect Spirit" rule. For the chart in question, it is permissible to have water at *zhen*.

Fig-5c: A Period-7 property sitting *ren* facing *bing* violates "Hidden Siren" (8-8) at *gen* palace, which is neither the Sitting nor the Facing palace. There is nothing much to be feared as Star-8 represents growth *qi* in Period-7, i.e. timely, and will in fact become prosperous in the next Period.

Even if the Star is not timely, all it takes is open space outside *gen* palace to resolve the problem. Moreover, any problem arising from this "Siren" will only affect the 3rd son, a young male or a *gua*-8 person. If no such person resides in the property, there is nothing to worry about.

Fig-5d: A Period-7 property sitting *jia* facing *geng* has a more serious problem. The Sitting Stars violate "Hidden Sirens" at all 9 palaces (全盤伏吟). The Facing Star at *zhen* palace also violates "Inverse Siren". It is of course an "Up Mountain Down Water" chart.

Such a chart is difficult to deal with, and if in addition the property is hemmed in on all sides by sheer cliffs or a concrete jungle, the only advice to give is: Run!

Line SX10 says a household violating "Hidden Siren" will not have natural offspring and will have to depend on adopted children to continue the family line. In this modern day and age, we need not be that pessimistic. [The old masters obviously have not heard of fertility drugs or in-vitro fertilization ☺]

> *In the old days, people observed that a certain species of hornets tended to carry to their nest life worms that were the larvae of the snout moth. They deduced that the hornets were unable to procreate naturally, and had to adopt the young moths as their own.*
>
> *So "moth larva" became a metaphor for an adopted child.*
>
> *Nowadays we know better. In fact the hornets brought home the worms to lay eggs on them, so that when the young hornets hatched, they had a ready supply of live feed.*
>
> *Nevertheless, the metaphor stuck.*

Chapter 2 – Summary

- A "Prosperous Sitting Prosperous Facing" chart is only good if the Sitting palace sees mountain and the Facing palace sees water. If the chart is not supported by the appropriate landforms, it is just a set of numbers.

- The Facing and Sitting Stars that are currently prosperous (Star-8 in Period-8) represent the husband and wife; and the future prosperous Stars (Stars-9 & 1 in Period-8) represent the children and grandchildren. The capabilities and filial piety of the future generations will depend on the landforms outside the palaces containing the future prosperous Stars.

- A landform (mountain or water) that straddles over 2 adjacent Mountains of the *luo pan* is said to be impure. It signals the possibility of a woman remarrying and bringing with her children from her previous marriage.

- A property that violates "Inverse/Hidden Sirens" affects progeny, and the occupants may have to resort to adoption.

Chapter 3
Some Conjunctions, Good & Bad

CHAPTER 3:
Some Conjunctions, Good & Bad

> **SX11:** 山風值而泉石膏肓。
>
> Mountain and wind produce persons incurably addicted to the wilderness.

"Mountain and wind" refers to the Star conjunction 8-4.

"... incurably addicted to the wilderness" is an idiom used to describe extreme nature lovers who forsake materialistic attractions to spend their time wandering in the wilderness.

When the Stars are timely, 8-4 produces lofty thinkers and philosophers, but when the Stars are out of timing, they turn out bitter and disillusioned misfits instead. These people feel their talent has been neglected, and roam the world criticizing everything and contributing nothing.

8-4 represents a conflict between Earth and Wood. Health wise, Star-8 relates to the backbone, fingers and toes, and Star-4 relates to "wind". Hence an untimely 8-4 also indicates arthritis and other ailments of the bone and tendons.

Chapter 3: Some Conjunctions, Good & Bad

> **SX12:** 午酉逢而江湖花酒。
>
> Horse meeting Rooster leads to itinerant pleasure seeking and drink.
>
> [章作：午酉逢而江湖花柳。
>
> Zhang's version: Horse meeting Rooster leads to itinerant pleasure seeking and sexually transmitted diseases.]

"Horse meeting Rooster" refers to the Star conjunction 9-7.

Star-9 represents Fire and Star-7 Metal, hence a potentially explosive conflict.

Another way of looking at it: 9 is Later Heaven Fire; 7 is Early Heaven Fire. Hence 9-7 represents an overdose of beauty, passion, etc.

In the language of Trigrams: 9 is *li* (young woman, happiness, eyes, heart, etc.); 7 is *dui* (young girl, talk, mouth, etc).

With all the imagery of beautiful women, passion, whatnot... the prognosis is pretty obvious.

The renowned writer Shen Zu Mian (沈祖綿) suggested that the potential chaos could be averted if the Period Star at the afflicted palace is Star-1 (Water). [I guess in practice excessive liquid intake can dampen one's passion... ☺]

[Shen Zu Mian (沈祖綿) was the son of Shen Zhu Reng (沈竹礽), the acknowledged founder of modern *xuan kong* Flying Stars. Although Shen Junior was an accomplished *xuan kong* master in his own right, and was accredited with the publication of the masterpiece "Shen's *xuan kong* Studies (沈氏玄空學)", it was difficult for him to break out from the shadow of his father's illustrious image.]

Chapter 3: Some Conjunctions, Good & Bad

> **SX13:** 虛聯奎壁，啓八代之文章。
>
> The Constellation "Emptiness" linking to the Constellations "Legs" and "Wall" will launch literary works through 8 generations.
>
> [章作：星聯奎壁，啓八代之文章。
>
> Zhang's version: The Constellation "Star" linking to... (the rest unchanged)]

"Emptiness (虛)", "Legs (奎)" and "Wall (壁)" are all names of Constellations in the ancient Chinese Zodiac called the "28-Constellations (二十八宿)".

Relating the "28-Constellations Plate" of the *luo pan* to the "24-Mountains Plate", "Emptiness" is located at *zi* (North, hence Star-1); "Legs" and "Wall" are located at *xu* and *qian* respectively (Northwest, hence Star-6).

Line SX13 therefore refers to the Star conjunction 1-6.

Star-1 stands for scholarship and high status. Star-6 stands for officialdom and power. Hence 1-6 represents highly successful officials of the imperial court (equivalent to present day cabinet ministers and very senior civil servants). Needless to say, this will only happen when one of the Stars is timely (Both 1 and 6 cannot be timely at the same time).

The phrase "through 8 generations" confounded many a writer, whereas in fact the phrase refers not to the length of time, but to the universal appeal of a piece of literature or legislation. See side-bar.

To cut a long story short, Line SX13 says that the Star conjunction 1-6, when timely, will produce highly respected officials whose writings and decisions will win universal accolade.

Chapter 3: Some Conjunctions, Good & Bad

In Master Zhang's version, he used the word "Star (星)" instead of "Emptiness (虛)". This led to much debate between scholars, as "Star" Constellation is located at *wu* on the "24-Mountains Plate" (South, hence Star-9).

Did Master Zhang mean a 9-6 conjunction? But 9-6 indicates a fierce conflict between Fire and Metal, hardly the stuff for literary genius!

Some writers concluded that Zhang's version contained a typo error: "Star (星)" should have read "Emptiness (虛)".

The famous poet Su Dong Po (蘇東坡) once paid tribute to the Tang Dynasty philosopher Han Yu (韓愈), saying that Han's exhortations to the Emperor explained the downfall of the 8 Dynasties.

Historically, there were 8 short-lived dynasties just before Tang. These were collectively called the "8 Dynasties (八代)". The arrogance of their rulers led to the rapid downfall of the regimes.

The word "代 \<dài\>" in this context may be translated as "generation" or "dynasty".

The original phrase was "... writings that revealed the downfall of the 8 Dynasties (文起八代之衰)". Line SX12 merely borrowed from this phrase.

This explanation given by the Taiwanese writer Zhong Yi Ming (鐘義明) helped to clarify the confusion of many writers before him.

Chapter 3: Some Conjunctions, Good & Bad

> **SX14:** 胃入斗牛，積千箱之玉帛。
>
> When the "Stomach (胃)" Constellation enters the "Dipper (斗)" and "Ox (牛)" Constellations, a thousand boxes of jade and silk will accumulate.

The "Stomach (胃)" Constellation resides at *you* on the "24-Mountains Plate", hence Star-7; whereas "Dipper (斗)" and "Ox (牛)" Constellations reside at *gen* and *chou*, hence Star-8.

The Star conjunction 7-8 represents Earth growing Metal. When the Stars are timely, this conjunction will enable fabulous wealth.

Chapter 3: Some Conjunctions, Good & Bad

SX15: 雞交鼠而傾瀉，必犯徒流。

> When Rooster meets with Rat and torrential water runs off to one side, one will surely be banished to faraway places.

Rooster resides at the West, hence Star-7. Rat resides at the North, hence Star-1

A 7-1 conjunction, though sentimental in terms of Metal growing Water, also projects the image of frigid metal in icy water. The traditional explanation is that if the Stars are untimely and exacerbated by a negative landform like a large river flowing away (Star-1 is Water), 7-1 indicates that the occupants are likely to be exiled.

There is a more colourful explanation: Star-7 represents young girls or fun loving women; Star-1 represents drink. If these Stars come together when they are out of timing, the guys will be "drowned" in drink and debauchery, and young girls will fall for much older men. In both cases, the family unit breaks down. If, in addition, water flows away outside the afflicted palace (flow must be copious), the affected persons are likely to be booted out of the family or run away from home.

Health wise, these Star conjunctions indicate illnesses of the ears and kidneys. If water drains away, they could also indicate hemorrhage, incontinence or involuntary emission of seminal fluid.

Chapter 3: Some Conjunctions, Good & Bad

> **SX16:** 雷出地而相衝，定遭桎梏。
>
> When Thunder emerges from the Earth and clashes with it, one will surely be put in shackles.

Thunder represents the Trigram *zhen*, hence Star-3. Earth represents the Trigram *kun*, hence Star-2.

A 3-2 conjunction is popularly called "Bull Fight Killing (鬥牛煞)". It represents a clash between Wood and Earth. The popular interpretation is arguments. But surely one won't get chained up for a domestic quarrel? [Or has Sadomasochism become so popular?]

Line SX16 seems to suggest something more sinister. Star-3 is personified by the legendary Chi You (蚩尤), a ruthless and cruel warlord. Star-2 is of course the ever accommodating earth. When Star-3 is untimely, it behaves like a bully, thug and bandit, unleashing terror on society (the earth). Having had enough, the placid earth wakes up and exerts its righteous authority. The bandit gets arrested and put in shackles...

Line SX16 warns of possible eruptions of terror when Star-3 is untimely. On a smaller scale, it warns of road accidents, beatings, and lightning strikes. Such unpleasant events only transpire if the Star conjunctions are corroborated by negative landforms, in particular deformed or damaged mountains outside the afflicted palace.

Chapter 3: Some Conjunctions, Good & Bad

Chapter 3 – Summary

➢ Star conjunctions provide indications of likely outcomes. They form the basis of *xuan kong* predictions. A favourable prediction requires the Stars to be timely and supported by external landforms. Conversely, a negative prediction will only come true if the Stars are untimely and the landforms unsupportive.

Important note: for a given Star conjunction, the text ignores the order of the Stars, i.e. 1-6 is treated the same way as 6-1; 3-7 as 7-3; etc.

➢ 8-4 produces thinkers and philosophers on the positive side, otherwise aimless wanderers.

➢ 9-7 warns of excessive indulgence in drink and sex.

➢ 1-6 envisions notable success in high office.

➢ 7-8 creates fabulous wealth.

➢ 7-1 points to banishment; alternatively drink, debauchery and running away.

➢ 3-2 unleashes acts of terror and punishment.

Chapter 4
Of Growth & Control

CHAPTER 4:
Of Growth & Control

SX17: 火剋金兼化木，數驚回祿之災。

Fire counters Metal and if Wood is formed in the process, there will be multiple fire scares.

[章作：火若剋金兼化木，數經回祿之災。

Zhang's version: If Fire counters Metal and Wood is formed in the process, multiple fire disasters will come to pass.]

Star-9 is fire; Star-7 is Metal. In addition, the Early Heaven number 7 also represents Fire. Hence 9-7 heightens the dangers of fire.

But why not 9-6? After all Star-6 is also Metal. All the writers focused on 9-7, quoting Early Heaven Fire in support. This Star conjunction is described at length in the "Purple White Script". 9-6 will be discussed separately.

The consequential formation of Wood is a matter of conjecture. Certain writers interpreted the phrase to mean the presence of Star-1 at the same palace. Their argument goes like this: Star-1 is *ren* Water; Star-9 is *ding* Fire. *ding* and *ren* combine to form Wood, based on the "Stem Combinations" theory. Wood fuels the Fire, hence the fire ignites.

Other writers argued that fires will only break out if there is Wood Star present.

Yet other writers disagreed. They said that 9-7 by itself is strong enough to ignite a fire, if the Period or Annual Star at the same palace is also Fire related (2, 7 & 9).

The popular version talks about multiple fire scares (驚 *<jing>*). Zhang's version says multiple fires will come to pass (經 *<jing>*). The 2 words are phonetically identical.

Chapter 4: Of Growth & Control

SX18: 土制水復生金，自主田莊之富。

Earth controls Water and also grows Metal. This naturally points to the wealth of the manor.

[章作：土能制水復生金，定主田莊之富。

Zhang's version: Earth is able to control Water and also grow Metal. This confirms the wealth of the manor.]

Earth refers to Stars-2 & 8; Water to Star-1; and Metal to Stars-6 and 7.

The majority of writers proffered the explanation that the Star conjunction 1-6 on meeting the Annual Star-2 or 8 will see a sentimental relationship of Earth growing Metal, and Metal growing Water. As Metal relates to wealth and Earth to the land, the prognosis is a wealthy landed property.

In fact the explanation could be expanded to include all cases of 3-Star conjunction that include an Earth Star (2, 8), a Water Star-1, and a Metal Star (6, 7), be they Sitting Star, Facing Star, Period Star, *luo shu* Star, Annual Star, physical water, whatever.

Shen Zu Mian (沈祖緜) cited the example described in Fig-6:

A Period-2 property sitting *wu* facing *zi* has Facing Star-2, Period Star-7 and *luo shu* Star-1 at *kan* palace. That would have given an Earth-Metal-Water conjunction. The physical water merely reinforced the conjunction.

Zhang's version is semantically the same.

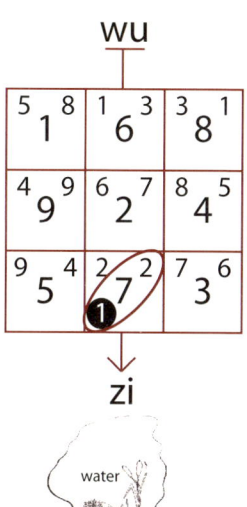

Fig-6: 2-7-1 combo

Secrets of Xuan Kong 39

Chapter 4: Of Growth & Control

> **SX19:** 木見火而生聰明奇士。
>
> When Wood sees Fire, astonishingly intelligent persons will be born.

Wood refers to Star-3 or 4; and Fire refers to Star-9.

Line SX19 says a 3-9 or 4-9 conjunction indicates intelligent persons.

As with the previous Line, the Stars can come in any form: Sitting, Facing, Period, *luo shu*, whatever.

These Star conjunctions give rise to the idiom: "Wood enables the fire to burn bright (木火通明)", often used to describe intelligent kids in a household.

Chapter 4: Of Growth & Control

> **SX20:** 火見土而出愚鈍頑夫。
>
> When Fire sees Earth, stupid and stubborn clods will emerge.

Fire refers to Star-9; Earth refers to Star-2 or 8.

Going strictly by the text, a 9-2 or 9-8 conjunction would produce idiots. This is not borne out in practice. After all, Fire produces Earth. The conjunction is sentimental, unless there is excessive Fire, in which case the saying "Intense fire scorches the earth (火炎土燥)" comes into play.

Various writers have pointed out that the prognosis is applicable only if the Stars are out of timing and exacerbated by oppressive mountains.

Chapter 4: Of Growth & Control

> **SX21:** 無室家之相依，奔走於東西道路。
>
> Devoid of family support, one rushes about on the east west highway.

There are different explanations:

(a) The more popular explanation has this to say: For a Flying Stars chart to be effective, the Facing Star at the Facing palace needs to be supported by water, or at least low ground; and the Sitting Star at the Sitting palace should be backed by a mountain or high ground. In this way, the Stars are said to have family support. Conversely, if the required landforms are not in place, the Stars are said to be devoid of family support.

A chart that is not properly supported by landforms indicates that the occupants may be busy all the time, but the results are not commensurate with the effort.

(b) Some writers took the view that the words "east west" refer to Star-3 and Star-7. That is to say, the conjunction 3-7, if not property supported, indicates toil without commensurate rewards.

3-7 becomes a Later Heaven combination (Combo-10) only if the Stars are supported. Otherwise they indicate a Wood-Metal conflict.

(c) Master Zhang took a more holistic view. He explained that Lines SX17 ~ SX22 taken together underscored the need to balance the interaction between Elements according to the principle of supporting the weak and dissipating the strong.

He said that *yin* and *yang* needed each other to form a cohesive unit, the family. Either one without the other would lead to loneliness, hence the term "devoid of family support". The end result would be ineffectual actions such as "rushing about on the east west highway" (Line SX21) and "seeking shelter and food at other peoples' homes" (Line SX22).

yin and *yang* are to be taken in the widest possible sense, including mountain/water; dense/sparse; passive/active; and the list goes on…

Chapter 4: Of Growth & Control

> **SX22:** 鮮姻緣之作合，寄食於南北人家。
>
> The newly married couple seeks shelter and food at other people's homes to the south and north.

"Newly married couple" clearly refers to *yin* and *yang*. "Seeking shelter and food at other peoples' homes" is another way of saying the couple cannot afford their own home. In other words, the union is deficient and procreation becomes difficult.

In rhythmic structure, Line SX22 makes a perfect response to Line SX21 above.

Zhang's holistic view as explained in Line SX21 is profound but not very practical.

One interpretation is that the line is an oblique reference to the principle of *xuan kong's* "Castle Gate Formula (城門訣)". It implies that if the required water is not found at the property's facing but there is a channel for *qi* to enter from one of the palaces to the side, then wealth is still in the offing (see Appendix-2). The explanation sounds rather farfetched to me, but surprisingly *xuan kong* heavyweights like Shen Zu Mian (沈祖綿) and Kong Zhao Su (孔昭蘇) went for it.

Other writers took the view that "south and north" refers to Stars-9 & 1, and also the Trigrams *li* and *kan*. 9-1 makes up a Combo-10 when the Stars are supported. Otherwise it represents a Fire-Water clash.

When the Stars are untimely, the water dries up, alternatively spills over out of control. The Trigram *li* has one broken line between 2 solid lines, i.e. empty inside. The prognosis is inability to conceive or a miscarriage.

Chapter 4: Of Growth & Control

Chapter 4 – Summary

➢ 9-7 stands for enhanced fire risk, especially if a Wood Star is present to feed the Fire.

➢ 2-1-7, 8-1-6, etc., (Earth-Water-Metal) enables property related wealth.

➢ 3-9, 4-9 are signs of intelligent persons.

➢ 9-2, 9-8 indicate stupidity.

➢ 3-7 unsupported suggests rushing about with little achievement.

➢ 9-1 unsupported makes procreation difficult.

Chapter 5
Man & Woman

CHAPTER 5:
Man & Woman

> **SX23:** 男女多情，無媒妁則爲私約。
>
> The man and woman are amorous, but without a matchmaker, they can only meet surreptitiously.
>
> [章作：男女多情，無媒妁則爲私合。
>
> Zhang's version: The man and woman are amorous, but without a matchmaker, their marriage will be improper.]

"Man and woman are amorous" refers to beautiful mountains and water, i.e. landform *fengshui* (巒頭). "Matchmaker" refers to the correct application of *qi* management techniques (理氣) such as establishing the correct orientation, ensuring the Stars are timely, etc.

Line SX23 says that superior landforms on their own are not enough. Without *qi* management, the desired results cannot be obtained.

Zhang's version is more or less the same. He just took it a bit further: from an exploratory dating experience to a wedding Las Vegas style!

Chapter 5: Man & Woman

> **SX24:** 陰陽相見，遇冤仇而反無冤。
>
> When *yin* sees *yang*, any animosity will be rendered harmless.
>
> [章作：陰陽相見，遇冤仇則反無情。
>
> When *yin* sees *yang*, any animosity will turn merciless.]

This Line has generated much debate amongst writers. Zhang's version appears to contradict the popular version. The controversy is centred on the last 2 words: whether they should in fact be "無冤 (without animosity)"; "無情 (merciless)"; or "無猜 (no doubt)". Typo errors were common in 19th Century publications.

The 2 possible explanations are:

(a) If mountain and water are correctly positioned and the Stars are timely, any supposed conflict between Star elements will be rendered harmless;

(b) Even if mountain and water are both present, an "Up Mountain Down Water" chart will turn the situation merciless.

In either case, the message is that landforms and *xuan kong* Stars should be evaluated together.

Line SX24 merely echoes Line SX23 above. You guessed it: the 2 lines make up a couplet.

Chapter 5: Man & Woman

> **SX25:** 非正配而一交，有夢蘭之兆。
>
> The union of a man with a woman other than his principal wife may yet beget the oracle of "lily in a dream" (idiom meaning pregnancy)
>
> [章作：惟正配而一交，有夢蘭之兆。
>
> Only the union of a man with his principal wife can beget the oracle of "lily in a dream" (idiom meaning pregnancy)]

The idiom "lily in a dream" refers to the conception and birth of a child destined for greatness. See sidebar.

Let's first deal with the popular version: In the times when polygamy was the norm, the children born of the principal wife had privileges over the other children. They were always accorded the best opportunities.

What Line SX25 appears to say is that children born of the secondary wives could be just as capable.

Stars-6 & 2, 3 & 4, 1 & 9, 8 & 7 are regarded as natural pair bonding based on the *luo shu* family relationships. These Star conjunctions are regarded as pair bonding between a man and his principal wife. They are capable of delivering positive outcome, if the Stars are supported by the appropriate landforms.

Star conjunctions like 1-2, 2-3, 6-7, 8-9 are also *yin-yang* pairs, though not the natural pairs. These are likened to the union between a man and his secondary wives. Line SX25 says such conjunctions are no less capable of positive outcome as long as the Stars are supported.

Chapter 5: Man & Woman

Zhang took a different view. According to him, only natural pairs are positive.

Strangely, in his annotations he commented on Lines SX23, SX24 and SX26, all in one breath, but left out SX25.

Shen Zu Mian (沈祖綿) went down a different route. According to him, the line refers to the "Castle Gate Formula" of *xuan kong*. Principal wife refers to a prosperous Star at the Facing palace, and secondary wife refers to water at one of the adjacent palaces.

In other words, if the property is unable to benefit directly from the Facing palace, the "Castle Gate Formula" provides an alternative source of wealth *qi*. See Appendix-2 for a discussion on the "Castle Gate Formula".

> In the "Spring-Autumn Period" of Chinese history (770~476BCE), the Duchy of Zheng (鄭國) was a small state sandwiched between powerful neighbours.
>
> One night a concubine of the Duke of Zheng by the name of Yan Ji (燕姞) had a dream in which an angle appeared offering her a stalk of lily flower, saying the flower represented a child destined for greatness.
>
> Soon after that, Yan Ji conceived and in due course gave birth to a son. She named him Lily (蘭). Just imagine what the boy had to endure with a name like that!
>
> At the time, children of concubines were not regarded highly in the social pecking order and seldom featured in the line of succession, but by a twist of fate, Lily did in fact become the next Duke of Zheng. He took the reign name "Duke Mu of Zheng (鄭穆公, 627~606BCE)".
>
> By dexterous diplomacy and subterfuge when necessary, Duke Mu steered his Duchy through troubled times and managed to keep his predatory neighbours at bay.
>
> In memory of this great ruler who rose above his lowly position at birth, the idiom "lily in a dream" was coined to describe a pregnancy that held great promise.

Chapter 5: Man & Woman

> **SX26:** 得干神之雙至，多折桂之英。
>
> The arrival of "Stem Gods" in pairs will produce many distinguished persons who will "break the cassia twigs" (idiom meaning academic success).

Note that Line SX26 is the response to Line SX25 in couplet style.

The idiom "break the cassia twigs" refers to outstanding success at the public exams. See sidebar.

The term "Stem Gods arriving in pairs" is nebulous. None of the explanations provided by various writers is totally convincing.

Perhaps Shen Zu Mian's (沈祖綿) explanation makes the most sense. He said that if the Facing and Sitting Stars are both prosperous, and if the supporting landforms are duplicated, i.e. there is another expanse of water beyond the first at the Facing, and one mountain behind another at the Sitting, then the property is likely to produce highly intelligent and successful scholars.

In Imperial China, public exams were conducted periodically to recruit scholars into the civil service.

When the exam results were announced, the top scorers had a tradition of breaking off twigs from a cassia (a type of cinnamon) tree.

We're not quite sure what they did with the twigs, but a headgear made of cassia twigs was mentioned in a 3rd Century poem as a symbol of exalted morality, albeit that was in a different context.

The practice had a parallel in ancient Greece and Rome where laurel wreaths were placed on the heads of winners and poets, and I suppose the modern equivalent would be Nobel Laureates.

From Tang Dynasty (7th Century CE) onwards, the phrase "to break the cassia twigs" was used to describe successful candidates at the highest level of public exams (進士).

Chapter 5: Man & Woman

> **SX27:** 陰神滿地成群，紅粉場中空快樂。
>
> When a group of *yin* Stars converge on the land, the arena of red powder will be the scene of pointless revelry.
>
> [章作：陰神滿地成群，紅粉場中快活。
>
> Zhang's version says almost the same thing except the word "pointless" is omitted.]

The common interpretation is that "*yin* Stars" refers to Stars-2, 4, 7 & 9 (female family members); and "red powder" is a metaphor for heavy makeup, meaning womenfolk.

By this interpretation, Line SX27 says that if a group of 3 "female" Stars gathers at one palace, the womenfolk will have a field day. If the Stars are timely, the convergence indicates women holding the reins of power; if untimely it means the women seek wanton pleasures. [In traditional Chinese culture, it was ok for the guys to be promiscuous, but never the girls. Any form of sex other than for the purpose of procreation was considered wanton pleasures ☹]

Fig-7 shows a Period-3 property sitting *geng* facing *jia*, where Stars-4, 9 & 2 reside at *xun* palace; and Stars-2, 7 & 9 at *kun*. In Period-3, only Star-4 was timely. The prognosis could be that the eldest daughter called the shots, while the mother tended to be irresponsible. Of course such a prognosis would only be valid if the landforms were consistent.

However, I have my doubts whether that interpretation is correct, and I am not alone in that. If Lines SX27 and SX28 are read together, the following interpretation seems more reasonable:

"*yin* Stars" refers passive Stars, i.e. the ones out of timing. Line SX27 therefore says that when there is an abundance of passive Stars at one palace, people associated with that palace, both men and women, will tend to spend their time

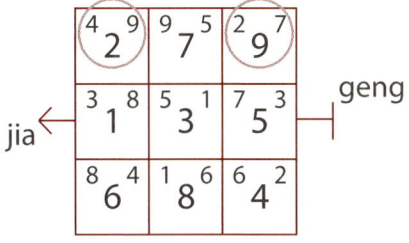

Fig-7: *yin* Stars converge

unproductively at pleasure seeking venues. [It should be pointed out that these so-called "houses of ill repute" were legitimate establishments in those days. Could have been great fun! Only prudes and those who felt threatened would turn their noses up at such places ☺]

Secrets of Xuan Kong

Chapter 5: Man & Woman

> **SX28:** 火曜連珠相值，青雲路上自逍遙。
>
> When Fire Stars meet in a pearl chain, the road to the "azure clouds" will be smooth and easy.
>
> [章作：火曜聯珠相遇，青雲路上逍遙。
>
> Zhang's version: slightly different words but the same meaning.]

The common interpretation of "Fire Star" is a mountain with a pointed tip like a Chinese writing brush, or several pointed peaks in a row reminiscent of a scholar's brush rest. "Pearl chain" refers to the Star conjunctions 1-6, 2-7, 3-8, 4-9, 9-1 and 1-4. The first 4 are *he tu* combinations; whereas 9-1 and 1-4 are other conjunctions that indicate the might of the pen.

"Azure clouds" is a metaphor for high status and reputation earned through the public exams.

Hence if there is a Fire shaped mountain outside a palace having the Star conjunctions mentioned above, a smooth and easy ride to status and fame is assured.

One problem with this interpretation is that Lines SX27 and SX28 appear disconnected. As the lines are 2 parts of a couplet, one would have expected them to be complementary in meaning as well as in words.

My preference is for an alternative interpretation, as follows:

If "*yin* Stars" in Line SX27 refers to the passive untimely Stars, "Fire Stars" should refer to the active timely Stars. "Fire" alludes to "brightness", a figurative description of the timely Stars.

"Meet in a pearl string" does not refer to 3 sequential numbers. It is merely a play of words to suggest the meeting of several "bright" Stars at one palace. [The other explanation that "pearl string" refers to 1-6, 2-7, etc. does not hold water. Since when was a string ever made up of only 2 pearls?]

Chapter 5: Man & Woman

Moreover, the expressions "group of *yin* Stars converge" (Line SX27) and "Fire Stars meet in a pearl chain" (Line SX28) match perfectly in rhythmic structure.

In other words, Line SX28 states that when there are multiple timely Stars at a palace, the persons related to that palace will be driven by positive ambition, which is the opposite of spending unproductive time at entertainment outlets. Again the rhythmic match is perfect.

In both Lines SX27 and SX28, the need for appropriate landforms to support the prognoses goes without saying.

Chapter 5: Man & Woman

> **SX29:** 非類相從，家多淫亂。
>
> Different types following one another will likely lead to unrestrained lust in the family.

Different types of what?

2 explanations have been tendered:

(a) 1-9, 2-6, 3-4, 7-8 make up the natural *yin/yang* pairs. All other *yin/yang* pairs are considered "different types" (according to Bao Shi Xuan (鮑士選) and co);

(b) The "Prosperous Sitting Prosperous Facing" chart has to be supported by the correct landforms, otherwise it constitutes "different types", and the outcome may not be beneficial (according to Shen Zu Mian (沈祖綿) and co).

I am not convinced by either.

In Line SX25, we were told that the less than perfect *yin-yang* pairs are also capable of producing offspring of distinction. So why sing a different tune now?

Shen's version sounds like a broken record. Every time when a line is ambiguous, he fell back to his favorite tune.

On the face of it, "different types" can mean a mixture of timely and untimely Stars, but then such mixtures are very common indeed, in fact more the rule than the exception. Is unrestrained lust that common?

I take the view that Lines SX27~SX30 should be read as a group, and the latter 2 lines are just a reiteration of the former 2, in broad terms. Do take note of the indisputable links between "red powder" in Line SX27 and "unrestrained lust" in Line SX29; and between "azure clouds" in Line SX28 and "good and virtuous persons" in Line SX30.

We don't have to think that wondrous secrets are hidden within each and every line of the text.

Chapter 5: Man & Woman

SX30: 雌雄配合，世出賢良。

A properly matched pair of female and male will bring forth good and virtuous persons into this world.

[章作：雌雄相合，世出賢良。

Zhang's version uses a different word, but the meaning is unchanged.]

Here again the various annotations tended to be wishy-washy, talking about the *yin/yang* polarities of mountain and water.

I shall stick with my helicopter view of Lines SX27~SX30. See comment under Line SX29.

Chapter 5: Man & Woman

Chapter 5 – Summary

- Landforms must be evaluated together with the 9 Stars.

- 6-2, 3-4, 1-9, 8-7 are the natural pairs based on the *luo shu* family relationships, but any other pair made up of a male Star (6, 3, 1, 8) and a female Star (2, 4, 9, 7) is also good for progeny purposes.

- Duplicated landforms produce highly intelligent and successful scholars.

- Multiple (3 or more) untimely Stars gathered at one palace indicate people immersed in unproductive activities.

- Multiple timely Stars stand for positively driven achievers.

Chapter 6
Ushering in Wealth

CHAPTER 6:
Ushering in Wealth

SX31: 棟入南離，驟見廳堂再煥。

With a column (of wood) entering Southern *li*, one rapidly sees the reception hall lighting up again.

[章作：負棟入南離，佇見廳堂更煥。]

Zhang's version: With a column (of wood) moving into Southern *li*, one stands by waiting for the reception hall to light up again.]

"Column of wood" refers to Star-3; "Southern *li*" to Star-9.

Wood grows Fire. Wood relates to scholarship, Fire to fame. When one becomes successful and well known, one is bound to have many visitors. Hence the reception hall is lit up constantly. The transformation from Wood to Fire is quick, hence rapid fame/wealth.

For wealth and worldly gains, the 3-9 conjunction should involve the Facing Star, and the presence of water is required.

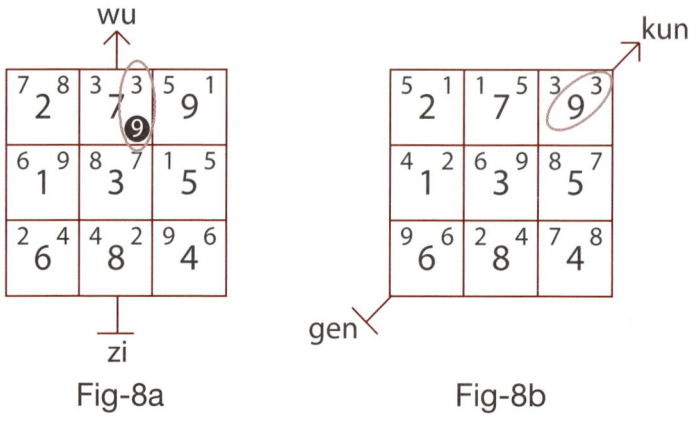

Fig-8: 3-9 combo

Fig-8 shows 2 examples. In Fig-8a, Facing Star-3 arrives at *li* palace (*luo shu* Star-9). The 3-9 conjunction is between Facing Star and *luo shu* Star. In Fig-8b, the conjunction is between Facing Star-3 and Period Star-9 at *kun* palace.

Chapter 6: Ushering in Wealth

> **SX32:** 車驅北闕，時聞丹詔頻來。
>
> With the carriage at the North gate, one often listens to "crimson rulings" (idiom meaning imperial edicts) one after another.
>
> [章作：驅車朝北闕，時聞丹詔頻來。
>
> With the carriage facing the North gate, one often listens to "crimson rulings" (idiom meaning imperial edicts) one after another.]

In some old texts, *kun* (坤) is likened to a carriage.

The Emperor's decrees were written in red ink. Hence "crimson rulings" became a metaphor for imperial edicts. To be regularly apprised of such high level decisions, one had to be a minister or similar high ranking official.

"Carriage" refers to Star-2; "North gate" to Star-1 and also water; and Emperor to Star-6.

In other words, if Stars-2, 1 & 6 meet at a certain palace, and water is present, a person is destined for high office. 1-6 is a *he tu* combination; 6-2 makes up a father-mother pair, also the highly auspicious "Unity (泰)" Hexagram; and 1-2 (*kan* & *kun*) bears an Early/Later Heaven relationship. With such harmony and strong bonding between the Stars, exceedingly good fortune is in the offing.

Fig-9 shows an example. In a Period-7 property sitting *xin* facing *yi*, the 6-2-1 conjunction occurs at *gen* palace. It should be noted that the chart is "Prosperous Sitting Prosperous Facing", on top of which any water or road junction at *yin* (within *gen* palace) would be a "Direct Castle Gate" (see Appendix-2). It is indeed a superlative chart.

Note that the 3 Stars need not be restricted to Sitting, Facing and Period. The *luo shu*, Annual, landform, and other Stars are just as usable.

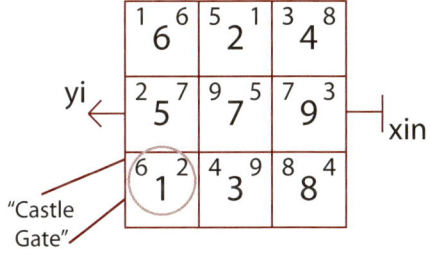

Fig-9: 6-2-1 conjunction

Chapter 6: Ushering in Wealth

> **SX33:** 苟無生氣入門，糧艱一宿。
>
> If no *sheng qi* enters the door, there will hardly be enough grain for one night.
>
> [章作：全無生氣入門，糧寒一宿。
>
> Zhang's version: Different words but the same meaning.]

"*sheng qi*" in this instance refers to the timely Stars. "Not enough grain for one night" is akin to the modern saying "not knowing where the next meal comes from".

Line SX33 says if the Facing Star is untimely, and there is no usable "Castle Gate", then the occupants will endure abject poverty.

A dire prognosis indeed, but in reality, how many families have we seen that have lost their livelihood just by living in a house with an untimely Star at the door? Let's be realistic.

Old texts have a tendency to exaggerate. I wonder why. People in the old days could have less access to education, but surely they were no less intelligent? Moreover, only educated people would read texts like this. So whom were they kidding?

Chapter 6: Ushering in Wealth

> **SX34:** 會有旺星到穴，富積千鐘。
>
> If the prosperous Star arrives at the "Spot", accumulated wealth will be worth a thousand bells.
>
> [章作：會有旺星到穴，富積千箱。
>
> Zhang's version: If the prosperous Star arrives at the "Spot", wealth will fill a thousand boxes.]

Technically, a "Spot" is the focal point of *qi* in an area, i.e. the precise location where the *qi* is strongest. In colloquial usage, the word also describes the inside of a dwelling, be it a grave or a house.

Having the prosperous Star at the Facing palace is not enough. Water must be present to enable the *qi* to coagulate and find its way into the dwelling. Note the text says prosperous Star arriving at the "Spot", not just at the door.

Here again, will one become rich just by having the prosperous Star at the Facing palace? Are all houses having "Prosperous Sitting Prosperous Facing" charts wealthy?

The tendency of old texts to exaggerate rears its head again.

Chapter 6: Ushering in Wealth

Chapter 6 – Summary

- 3-9 brings rapid fame and wealth.
- 2-1-6 signals high office.
- An untimely Facing Star without "Castle Gate" to help leads to abject poverty (exaggeration?)
- A timely Facing Star assisted by water means wealth (exaggeration?)

Chapter 7
To Redeem a Clash

CHAPTER 7:
To Redeem a Clash

SX35: 相剋而有相濟之功，先天之乾坤大定。
Two opposing entities can in fact be mutually supportive, as determined by Early Heaven *qian* and *kun*.

SX36: 相生而有相凌之害，後天之金木交併。
Two entities in a growth relationship can also be intimidating, as in the Later Heaven crossing of Metal and Wood.

Lines SX35 & SX36 should be read together. The 2 lines examine certain relationships between the 2 arrangements of the 8-Trigrams known as "Early Heaven" and "Later Heaven". These arrangements are shown in Fig-10 below:

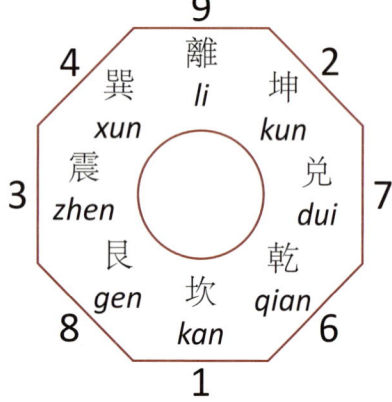

"Early Heaven" arrangement   "Later Heaven" arrangement

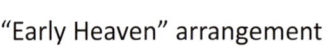

Fig-10: Early Heaven, Later Heaven

According to the 8-Trigrams theory, first there was the "Early Heaven" arrangement which represented the universe in perfect harmony. This then evolved into the "Later Heaven" arrangement which represented the imperfect world we live in today.

Chapter 7: To Redeem a Clash

The Stars 1 to 9 are closely integrated with the "Later Heaven" arrangement, to the extent that a Star number and its associated Trigram name are used interchangeably, for example: Star-1 is synonymous with *kan*; Star-2 with *kun*; etc.

Fig-10 shows that Star-9, aka *li*, used to be *qian* in the "Early Heaven" arrangement. In a manner of speaking, *li* came from *qian*. Similarly, Star-1, aka *kan*, can be said to have come from *kun*.

By right, Star-1 (*kan*, Water) should counter Star-9 (*li*, Fire), but *li* and *kan*'s "Early Heaven" counterparts, *qian* and *kun* (Heaven & Earth), are in perfect harmony. Hence *li* and *kan*, aka 9-1, should also be mutually supportive.

[The classic "Speaking of Hexagrams (說卦傳)" says:

Heaven and Earth set the locations	天地定位
Mountain and Marsh pass the *qi* between them	山澤通氣
Thunder and Wind are mutually attracted	雷風相薄
Water and Fire do not shoot at each other	水火不相射

The verse describes the Early Heaven arrangement of the 8 Trigrams, and also defines the non adversarial relationship between *kan* (Water) and *li* (Fire). Although they appear to be in opposition, the 2 are in fact mutually supportive, as both are needed to sustain life on earth.]

Let us next look at Star-3 (*zhen*, Wood) and Star-7 (*dui*, Metal). Their "Early Heaven" counterparts are *li* and *kan*, respectively. Whereas *li* in "Early Heaven" gives rise to *zhen* in "Later Heaven", and *kan* similarly gives rise to *dui*, "Later Heaven" *zhen* and *dui*, aka 3-7, are adversarial by nature.

The phrase "... growth relationship" in Line SX36 is ambiguous. Does it refer to *li* giving rise to *zhen* and *kan* giving rise to *dui*? To me, calling that a "growth relationship" is rather perverse, but then old texts are not known for their logical exactitude. Rhythmic balance was more important to them.

But what does all that Trigram theory mean in the context of Star conjunctions?

Several writers explained that Lines SX35 and SX36 exemplify the oft quoted statement: "Early Heaven becomes the body, Later Heaven becomes the application (先天為體, 後天為用)". To me, that's of little help.

A more practical interpretation would be that 9-1 is not usually adversarial unless the Stars are untimely and provoked by negative landforms.

On the other hand, 3-7 is usually in conflict. A beneficial 3-7 Later Heaven combination (Combo-10) can only materialize when one Star is timely (for 7 and 3 cannot be timely simultaneously) and supported by landforms. Other than that, the Stars are engaged in destructive Wood-Metal conflict.

Chapter 7: To Redeem a Clash

Take the case of a Period-7 property sitting *geng* facing *jia* (Fig-11).

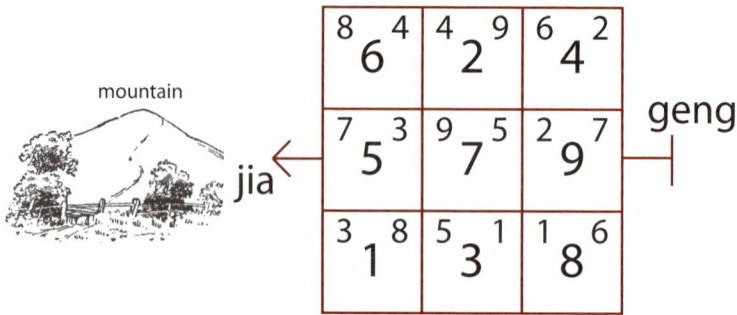

Fig-11: 7-3 at Facing

This is an "Up Mountain Down Water" chart, and in addition the Facing Stars violate "Hidden Siren" chart-wide.

That's pretty bad, but if the timely Sitting Star-7 at *zhen* (Facing palace) is supported by a mountain outside, then 7-3 at *zhen* may be read as a Combo-10, and that in a way redeems the chart.

Conversely, if there is water or open space outside *zhen* palace, a Combo-10 cannot form, and 7-3 represents a Metal-Wood conflict that further aggravates an already difficult chart.

This example illustrates how an "Up Mountain Down Water" chart can benefit from facing uphill.

Chapter 7: To Redeem a Clash

SX37: 木傷土而金位重重，雖禍有救。

Wood hurts Earth but at a location of multiple Metal, there is salvation to any mishap.

[章作：木傷土而金位重重，禍須有救。

Zhang's version: Different usage of words but largely the same meaning.]

"Wood hurts Earth" refers to the Star conjunctions 3-8, 4-8, 3-2, 4-2. If the Stars are untimely, mishaps are to be expected.

However, if the conjunction occurs at a palace where the Metal element is strong, then the wood is controlled by the Metal, which prevents it from hurting the Earth.

An example is when the Star conjunction occurs at *qian* or *dui* (Metal) palace, and the Period Star at the said palace happens to be 6 or 7 (both Metal). That would be considered a location of multiple Metal.

Fig-12 shows a Period-4 property sitting *gen* facing *kun*. The Sitting-Facing conjunction at *dui* is 5-8. On replacing 5 with the central Star-4, we have 4-8 which indicates the young male being hurt, but *dui* palace is Metal, and Period Star-6 at *dui* is also Metal. The multiple Metal saves the young male.

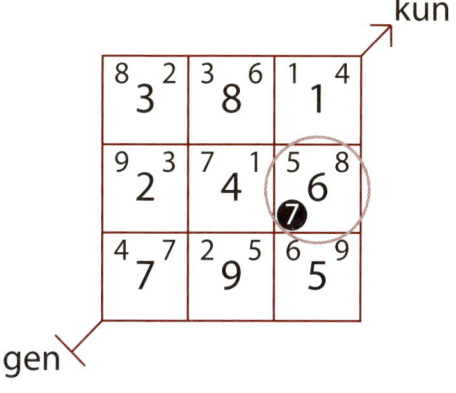

Fig-12: multiple Metal

Chapter 7: To Redeem a Clash

> **SX38:** 火剋金而水神疊疊，災不能侵。
>
> Fire controls Metal but with the Water god stacked up, disaster cannot invade.
>
> [章作：火制金而水神疊疊，災亦能禳。
>
> Zhang's version: Fire controls Metal but with the Water god stacked up, disaster can be warded off.]

"Fire controls Metal" refers to the Star conjunctions 9-6, 9-7. A Fire-Metal clash is often violent. 9-6 also stands for head ailment or a stroke; and 9-7 represents Later and Early Heaven Fire. When the Stars are out of timing, such disastrous occurrences are foretold.

Line SX38 says that if Water is strong, such as when the conjunction occurs at *kan* (Water) palace, and the Period Star at *kan* also happens to be 1, then there is no danger, as the Water would have dampened the Fire's ferocity.

Zhang's version says pretty much the same thing.

Chapter 7: To Redeem a Clash

SX39: 土困水而木旺，無妨。金伐木而火熒，何忌。

Earth traps Water but if Wood is prosperous, no harm. Metal cuts down Wood but if Fire dazzles, why worry?

[章作：土涸水而木旺，無妨。金伐木而火熒，無忌。

Zhang's version: Earth dries up the Water but if Wood is prosperous, no harm. Metal cuts down Wood but if Fire dazzles, no worries.]

This line is a follow-through from Lines SX37 and SX38 above. It is in fact 2 lines (a couplet) combined into one.

Earth (Stars-2, 5, 8) constrains Water (Star-1), but if Wood *qi* (Stars-3, 4) is vibrant, Earth's strength is compromised.

Likewise, Metal (Stars-6, 7) cuts wood (Stars- 3, 4), but if Fire *qi* (Star-9) is vibrant, Metal's aggressiveness is tempered.

The use of the terms "prosperous Wood (木旺)" and "dazzling Fire (火熒)" invokes the idea of timeliness. In other words, in Periods-3 & 4 (Wood), the Star conjunctions 2-1, 5-1, 8-1 are not to be viewed negatively. Likewise, in Period-9 (Fire), 6-3, 6-4, 7-3, 7-4 are harmless.

This merely underscores the need for *xuan kong* practitioners to be flexible and resourceful in interpreting the Stars and finding solutions to problems.

Stars from the Starting (*luo shu*) Plate; Period Plate; Sitting Plate; Facing Plate are just as usable. So are physical Mountain and Water Stars; Transformation Stars (1-6 to Water; 2-7 to Fire; 3-8 to Wood; 4-9 to Metal); and even people related Stars (for example, Star-2 for an elderly woman or a *gua*-2 person, etc.).

Chapter 7 – Summary

➢ 9-1 is usually not adversarial by virtue of its relationship with "Early Heaven" *qian-kun*.

➢ 3-7 is usually in opposition and will rarely form a Combo-10.

➢ 3-8, 4-8, 3-2, 4-2 all represent Wood hurting Earth, but if the conjunction occurs at a Metal palace and a Metal Star (6, 7) is also present, the conflict is resolved.

➢ 9-6, 9-7 represent a Fire-Metal conflict, but if the conjunction occurs at *kan* (Water) palace and Star-1 is also present, the situation is saved.

➢ 2-1, 8-1 represent Earth controlling Water, but if Wood (Stars-3, 4) is strong, no harm will come of it.

➢ 6-3, 6-4, 7-3, 7-4 represent Metal cutting Wood, but if Fire (Star-9) is prosperous, no worries.

Chapter 8
More of Growth & Control

Chapter 8: More of Growth & Control

CHAPTER 8:
More of Growth & Control

SX40: 吉神衰而忌神旺，乃入室而操戈。

When the beneficial gods are weak and the negative gods strong, one has to reach for a weapon upon entering the room.

[章作：忌神旺而制神弱，乃入室以操戈。

Zhang's version: When the negative gods are strong and the controlling gods weak, one has to reach for a weapon upon entering the room.]

SX41: 凶神旺而吉神衰，直開門而揖盜。

When the fearsome gods are strong and the beneficial gods weak, one is greeted by robbers upon opening the door.

[章作：吉神衰而凶神旺，直開門而揖盜。

Zhang's version: When the beneficial gods are weak and the fearsome gods strong, one is greeted by robbers upon opening the door.]

There appears to be a large degree of overlap between these 2 lines. The wording is ambiguous:

"Beneficial gods (吉神)" refers to Stars that grow or co-prosper the dominant Star. Of that there is little doubt;

Logically there is no clear distinction between "negative gods (忌神)" and "fearsome gods (凶神)". They both refer to Stars that control the dominant Star.

"Controlling gods (制神)" refers to the Stars that in turn control the "negative/fearsome gods". For example, if the dominant Star is Star-8 (Earth), Stars-3, 4 (Wood) would be the "negative/fearsome gods", and Stars-6, 7 (Metal) would be the "controlling gods" as Metal controls Wood.

A Star is strong if it is timely and supported by landforms. Likewise, a Star is weak when it is out-of-timing and unsupported.

Chapter 8: More of Growth & Control

"Reach for a weapon" and "greeted by robbers" should not be taken too literally. It simply implies that ill fortune will befall the residents of the affected property.

The contemporary writer Zhong Yi Ming (鐘義明) provided the following example that aptly illustrates the multi-faceted deliberations required of a *xuan kong* master. Rather lengthy, but well worth the patience to peruse:

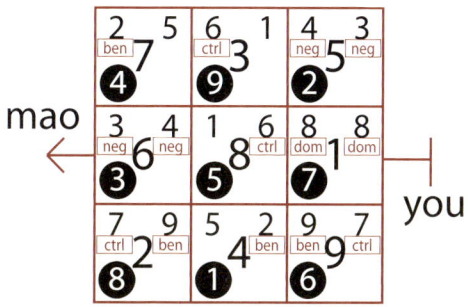

Fig-13: beneficial/negative/ controlling gods

Fig-13 shows a Period-8 property sitting *you* facing *mao* (alternatively sitting *xin* facing *yi*).

➤ In Period-8, Star-8 (Earth) is dominant. Stars-3, 4 (Wood) are "negative gods". Stars 6, 7 (Metal) control Wood and are therefore the "controlling gods". Star-9 (Fire) and Star-2 are "beneficial gods" as Fire grows Earth and Earth co-prospers Earth.

➤ In Period-8, Star-8 represents prosperous *qi*; Star-9 represents growth *qi*; Stars-6 & 7 represent retreating *qi*; Stars-3, 4 represent killing *qi*.

➤ Both Sitting Star-8 and Facing Star-8 (Earth) reside at *dui* palace. Although Star-8 is prosperous, its location at *dui* (*luo shu* Star-7, Metal) weakens the Earth, and Metal is in turn weakened by Period Star-1 (Water) at *dui*. The strength of Star-8 is therefore seriously impaired.

➤ Stars-3, 4 (Wood) are "negative gods" to the dominant Star-8 (Earth). Being Wood Stars, their presence at the Facing palace, *zhen* (Wood), strengthens them considerably. Although the Period Star-6 (Metal) at *zhen* is supposedly a "controlling god", Star-6 represents retreating *qi* in Period-8, and is powerless to control strong Wood.

Secrets of Xuan Kong

Chapter 8: More of Growth & Control

- If, in addition, there is a large river or mountain outside *zhen* lending strength to the "negative gods", it would be a classic case of "reaching for a weapon upon entering the room" or "greeted by robbers upon opening the door".

- If, on the other hand, the "Incoming Dragon" originates from *qian*, enters at *dui*, and is supported by a "Ghost Mountain", then the Sitting Star-9 ("beneficial god") at *qian* and Sitting Star-8 (prosperous) at *dui* would be greatly reinforced. If in addition there is an elegant mountain outside *li*, Sitting Star-6 ("controlling god") and *luo shu* Star-9 ("beneficial god") at *li* would also be empowered. These landforms would strengthen the chart enough to warrant a positive prognosis instead.

    ["Incoming Dragon" and "Ghost Mountains" are terms that describe landform entities. Please consult landform fengshui books for more info. For our present purpose, it would suffice to say that a "Ghost Mountain" is a small hill located behind the main mountain at the rear of the subject property. It is a desirable feature as it indicates that the "Incoming Dragon" has superior *qi*.]

- Alternatively, if the river enters from *xun* and flows past, *zhen*, *gen* and *kan* to *qian*, then Facing Star-4 at *zhen* would combine with Facing Str-9 at *gen* to form Metal ("controlling god"), and Facing Star-2 at *kan* would combine with Facing Star-7 at *qian* to form Fire ("beneficial god"). This would also be enough to turn around the negative situation.

Whoever said Flying Stars are simple and straightforward?

Chapter 8: More of Growth & Control

SX42: 重重剋入，立見消亡。

Invaded by multiple negative entities, demise is imminent.

[章作：重重剋入，立見死亡。

Zhang's version: Same meaning.]

"Negative entities" would include negative landforms like ugly mountains and merciless water, as well as virtual Stars whose element controls the self element (so-called "control-in").

Although unstated, it is assumed the reference entities are the Facing Star at the Facing palace, and Sitting Star at the Sitting palace. Moreover, the said Stars have to be out-of-timing for the prognosis to be valid.

Line SX42 says that if the Facing or Sitting palace is unfortunate enough to see negative landforms, on top of which other "control-in" Stars fly in, then ill fortune will strike. Although the text mentions loss of life, financial demise should not be precluded if the Facing Star is afflicted.

Chapter 8: More of Growth & Control

> **SX43:** 位位生來，連添財喜。
>
> Supported by multiple growth entities, wealth and happiness are continually topped up.
>
> [章作：位位生來，連添喜氣。
>
> Zhang's version: Supported by multiple growth entities, joyous events will occur repeatedly.]

Line SX43 is the converse of Line SX42.

If the Facing Star at the Facing palace and Sitting Star at the Sitting palace are timely, and they meet with other Stars whose elements grow or co-prosper the self element; and are, in addition, supported by positive landforms like charismatic mountains and sentimental water, then the property and residents will be blessed with abundant wealth and happiness.

Chapter 8: More of Growth & Control

> **SX44:** 不剋我而我剋，多出鰥寡孤獨之人。
>
> If, instead of controlling inwards, the Stars are controlled by me (the reference Star), chances are people will be lonely as in the case of widows and widowers.
>
> [章作：不剋我而剋我同類，多鰥寡孤獨之人。
>
> Zhang's version: If the Stars do not control me (the reference Star) but control others of my species, chances are people will be lonely as in the case of widows and widowers.]

This line is the subject of much debate amongst scholars. Having read the annotations of no less than 6 writers, past and present, I have yet to find a satisfactory explanation that addresses the topic squarely. Some writers drew on excerpts from old classics that appear to be out of context; others merely regurgitated earlier writers' comments without shedding any new light. Clearly the topic is perplexing.

Whilst I do not claim to be any wiser than the others, let me "take the bull by the horns" and try to explain this line and the next in a somewhat simplistic way that is at least consistent with the earlier Lines SX42 & SX43.

Moreover, the popular version contrasts sharply with Master Zhang's version. Let us first address the popular version, which says that if a Star does not control me ("control-in") but instead I control the Star ("control-out"), then people will be lonely. The reference Star in this case should be the Sitting Star at the Sitting palace, as the line deals with people matters.

Just as "control-in" is certainly harmful when the reference Star is weak, "control-out" is also detrimental. When a Star is weak (out-of-timing and unsupported by landforms), any attempt at controlling another Star ("control-out") will only deplete the reference Star's reserves.

In a related *xuan kong* text, the "Purple White Script (紫白訣)", an incoming Star controlling the host Star ("control-in") is labeled as "Killing (殺)"; whereas an incoming Star being controlled by the host Star ("control-out") is labeled as "Dead (死)". "Dead" is supposed to harm people matters but not wealth.

If the reference Star, in this case the Sitting Star at the Sitting palace, is out-of-timing and unsupported, and if other "control-out" Stars reside at the same palace, then the reference Star is so badly depleted that people luck suffers, to the extent that loneliness results.

Chapter 8: More of Growth & Control

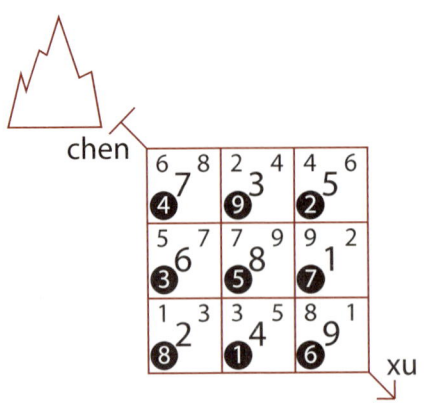

Fig-14: "control-out"

Fig-14 shows a Period-8 property facing *xu* sitting *chen*. The chart is "Up Mountain Down Water", with Sitting Star-6 (Metal) at the Sitting palace *xun*. Star-6 is out-of-timing in Period-8. Its location at *xun* also violates "Inverse Siren" (Appendix-1). If, in addition, there is a negative landform like a deformed mountain outside *xun*, our Sitting Star has a problem!

luo shu Star-4 (Wood) resides at *xun*. Star-6 has to deal with Star-4 (combo-10 cannot form because of the offending landform). If an additional Wood Star, say Annual Star-3 or 4, flies into *xun*, we have a situation of the Sitting Star being severely depleted.

Star-6 represents an elderly male. As his people luck goes down the drain, he risks losing his lifelong companion.

Next, we turn to Master Zhang's version which talks about "others of my species".

The contemporary writer Zhong Yi Ming (鐘義明) explained that in the Upper Cycle (Periods-1, 2, 3) Stars-1, 2, 3 are of the same species or members of the same family. Likewise in the Middle Cycle, Stars-4, 5, 6 are related; as are Stars-7, 8, 9 in the Lower Cycle.

For example, in Period-8, 9-7 (Fire controlling Metal) and 1-9 (Water controlling Fire) would be regarded as the same species, or members of the same family, being controlled.

However, Zhong failed to explain convincingly, at least not to me, why related Stars being controlled would produce lonely people.

Another writer, Ke Jian Cheng (柯建成), argued that "same species" and "members of the same family" refer to the timely Stars: i.e. in Period-8, Stars-8, 9, 1 are of the same species. He explained that if the other 2 timely Stars are under attack ("control-in"), future prosperity is at risk, hence loneliness. Neither would I buy this explanation.

Yet another writer, Shen Zu Mian (沈祖綿), even suggested that Zhang's version was his own fabrication. But then Shen is known to be highly opinionated and intolerant of divergent views.

Regrettably we shall have to walk away from this unresolved mystery.

Chapter 8: More of Growth & Control

> **SX45:** 不生我而我生，乃生俊秀聰明之子。
>
> If, instead of growing me, the Stars are grown by me, then one will produce attractive and intelligent children.
>
> [章作：不生我而生我家人，出俊秀聰明之士。
>
> Zhang's version: If the Stars do no grow me but grow members of my family, then one will produce attractive and intelligent children.]

Line SX45 is the converse of Line SX44. The 2 lines are also rhythmically matching.

First the popular version: it says that if the reference Star is not grown by the other Stars ("grow-in"), and instead the reference Star grows the others ("grow-out"), then one stands to beget elegant and bright offspring. Normally a "grow-out" relationship weakens the Star. Yet Line SX45 prescribes a positive outcome.

This can only be valid if the reference Star is strong, meaning it is timely and supported by positive landforms. A strong Star is able to withstand some degree of weakening or adversity. [Just as in ba zi, an overly strong self element needs to be weakened or clashed.]

Again, as the line deals with people matters, I take the position that the reference Star is the Sitting Star at the Sitting palace.

Why elegant and bright offspring? The idea could be that what the Star grows represents its children. If the Star is strong, it should produce quality children, or so the traditional concept goes, although genetically that is by no means certain. As the popular saying goes, "A tiger does not father a dog child (虎父無犬子)."

Here again, Master Zhang's version is markedly different. The controversy mentioned in the previous line applies equally here.

Chapter 8: More of Growth & Control

> **SX46:** 爲父所剋，男不招兒。
>
> If controlled by one's father, the male will be infertile.
>
> **SX47:** 被母所傷，女不成嗣。
>
> If hurt by one's mother, the female will be barren.
>
> [章作：爲母所傷，女難得嗣。
>
> Zhang's version: If hurt by one's mother, it is difficult for the female to conceive.]

These 2 deceptively simple lines are the subject of further controversy.

The following are 3 divergent interpretations:

- Shen Zu Mian (沈祖綿) & co. maintained that "father" refers to the Facing palace; and "mother" the Sitting palace. Further, "infertile male" refers to the absence of water at the 2 palaces adjacent to the Facing; and "barren female" refers to the absence of mountains at the 2 palaces adjacent to the Sitting. I find this explanation mildly amusing, if not outright ludicrous.

- Kong Zhao Su (孔昭蘇) & co. explained that both "father" and "mother" refer to the Sitting Star at the Sitting palace. Even if the Sitting palace is adequately supported by landforms, childlessness could still result if the Sitting Star is controlled by the dominant Star of the Period. Whilst this explanation is logical enough, it does not quite address the gender aspect of the 2 lines.

- Bao Shi Xuan (鮑士選) & co. ventured that "controlled by father" refers to the Star conjunctions 3-6, 4-6 (Star-6 being *yang* Metal); and "hurt by mother" refers to 3-7, 4-7 (Star-7 being *yin* Metal). Plausible but incomplete.

None of the above will survive rigorous cross-examination, which demonstrates once again the ambiguity of the original text.

Allow me to also throw my hat into the ring: the 2 lines set out to elaborate on the effects of a weak (untimely and unsupported) Sitting Star at the Sitting palace. If, in addition, the Sitting Star is controlled by another Star in the same palace, the chances of having children are indeed quite poor.

Chapter 8: More of Growth & Control

In the earlier part of the text (Line SX07), it was explained that timely Stars could be considered *yang*, and untimely Stars *yin*. Hence in Period-8, Stars-8, 9, 1 are *yang* (male, father, etc.), and the other Stars are *yin* (female, mother, etc.).

Taking this cue, "controlled by father" could mean the Sitting Star is controlled by a timely Star. For example, in Period-8, if Sitting Star-6 (Metal, untimely) is controlled by Star-9 (Fire, timely), then the prognosis is that the fertility problem lies with the male.

If, on the other hand, the Sitting Star is controlled by an untimely Star, it can be said to be "controlled by mother". For example, in Period-8, if Sitting Star-3 (Wood, untimely) is controlled by Star-7 (Metal, untimely), then it is the female who is unable to bear children.

This explanation may not be all that profound or sophisticated, but it cannot be faulted on logic. Of course such an explanation would have been hugely unpopular in the old days. When a couple was childless, the blame was always put on the woman, never the guy! In fact it was good enough reason for him to take on a 2nd wife, and a 3rd, and a 4th ... ☺

Chapter 8: More of Growth & Control

SX48: 後人不肖，因生方之反背無情。

If one's descendants are unworthy, it is because the landform mercilessly turns its back at a growth location.

The various writers are in agreement that "growth location", in this instance, is unrelated to "grow-in" or "grow-out". Instead it refers to the palaces at which the future prosperity Stars reside.

For example, in Period-8, Star-8 represents current prosperity, whereas Star-9 and Star-1 represent future prosperity. The palaces where these future prosperity Stars reside are called "growth locations".

Although Line SX48 does not specify the type of landform, it is reasonable to assume that as mountains affect people luck, it is the mountains turning away (i.e. instead of embracing the subject property, the hills turn outwards, sometimes called a "reverse embrace") at a "growth location" that will directly affect the quality of future generations.

By the same reckoning, it should be the Sitting Stars that govern people matters.

However, if merciless water (for example rushing water, reverse bow water, etc.) is found outside the palace where a future prosperity Facing Star resides, then it would be equally valid to predict that the family fortune will be squandered by later generations.

Fig-15 illustrates just such a case: Period-8 property sitting *gen* facing *kun*. Mountain range turns away at *zhen* (Sitting Star-9) indicates unfilial descendents. Water rushing straight out at *li* (Facing Star-9) indicates loss of family fortune.

The departing mountains at *zhen* also indicate that the eldest son is unworthy.

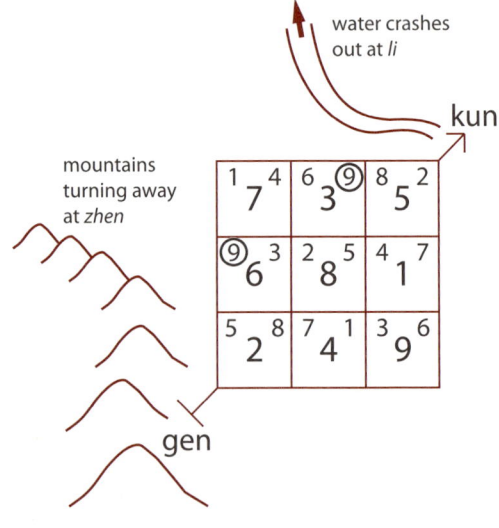

Fig-15: unworthy descendents

Chapter 8: More of Growth & Control

> **SX49:** 賢嗣承宗，緣生位之端拱朝揖。
>
> If one is blessed with virtuous descendents to continue the bloodline, it's attributable to the landforms bowing towards the growth location.
>
> [章作：賢嗣承宗，緣生位之端方朝揖。
>
> Zhang's version: Slightly different wording but same meaning.]

Line SX49 is a fitting response to Line SX48 in both style and content.

Here again, the key determinants are the mountain formations outside the palaces containing the future prosperity Stars, i.e. the "growth locations".

"Landforms bowing towards…" describes the mountains dropping down gently at the desired locations, conjuring up the image of a visitor greeting oneself with respect – clearly an auspicious sign.

[The traditional Chinese bow is to clasp both hands in front, head down, and bend forward at the waist. It is a gesture of respect to the other party.]

As the blessed sign is seen outside a "growth location", it behooves the descendants to be virtuous and capable.

Lines SX48 and SX49 clearly illustrate the concurrent use of Stars and landforms to make predictions in *xuan kong*.

Chapter 8: More of Growth & Control

> **SX50:** 我剋彼而反遭其辱，因財帛以喪身。
>
> I am supposed to control (exploit) an entity but am instead humiliated by that entity. That indicates loss of life for the sake of wealth.
>
> [章作：我剋彼而竟遭其辱，因財帛以喪身。
>
> Zhang's version: Same meaning.]

When the Facing Star at the Facing palace is timely, it needs to see water to realize its full potential as a wealth generator, irrespective of the Facing Star's element.

The word "control (剋)" in the present context should be interpreted to mean "exploit" or "make use of", rather than an elemental clash.

However, if the Facing Star is out-of-timing, its ability to exploit wealth opportunities is compromised. Line SX50 warns that a weak Facing Star could be so overwhelmed by the water that it figuratively "drowns". That would be analogous to excessive greed driving a man to his death.

[The idea is clearly borrowed from *ba zi*: the element I control is my wealth (我剋者爲財); and "too much wealth hurts the health (財多身弱)".]

Chapter 8: More of Growth & Control

SX51: 我生之而反被其災，爲難產以致死。

I am supposed to grow an entity but am instead distressed by that entity. That indicates difficulties in childbirth leading to death.

[章作：我生之而反受其殃，因產難而致死。

Zhang's version: Same meaning]

When the Sitting Star at the Sitting palace is timely, it needs to be supported by a mountain to optimize people luck, irrespective of the Sitting Star's element.

The word "grow (生)" in this context should be interpreted as "engender" or "bring about", rather than one element producing another.

If the Sitting Star is untimely, the mountain that is supposed to enable its procreative powers could in fact be overbearing, to the extent that the Star is exhausted and fails to deliver. In human terms, that would be equivalent to life threatening complications at childbirth.

Lines SX50 & SX51 use rather scary language, but if one think about it, the lines are merely a dramatic way to express what is a rather basic Flying Stars principle: that a property having an "Up Mountain Down Water" chart – where the Facing Star at the Facing Palace and Sitting Star at the Sitting palace are both untimely – should not sit with its back to a hill and face water in front.

As to whether the consequences are as dire as death from greed or childbirth, I think we should allow the author some poetic licence.

Chapter 9: Physical & Emotional Distress

Chapter 8 – Summary

- When Stars that grow or support the prosperous Star (beneficial Stars) are weak, but the Stars that control it (harmful Stars) are strong, misfortune is likely to strike. In that event, look for the Stars that control the harmful Stars in turn, for these are possible saviors.

- If the Sitting Star at the Sitting palace meets with multiple Stars that control it (harmful Stars), and on top of that there are negative landforms outside the palace, people matters will be gravely affected. Likewise wealth will be decimated if the Facing Star at the Facing palace is similarly afflicted.

- Conversely, if the said Stars meet with multiple Stars that grow or co-prosper with them, and the landforms are charismatic and sentimental, then abundant wealth and happiness are in the offing.

- If the Sitting Star at the Sitting palace is already weak and in addition it meets with Stars that it controls, then the Star's energy is depleted and people luck suffers.

- If the same Star is strong and it meets with Stars that it grows, then it is an indication of attractive and intelligent children.

- If an already weak Sitting Star at the Sitting palace meets with a Star that controls it, the outcome could be childlessness. If the controlling Star is timely, the infertility problem lies with the man. If the controlling Star is untimely, the problem lies with the woman.

- The palaces where the future prosperous Stars reside affect the behaviour of the descendants. Negative landforms outside those palaces point to the descendants not being filial or squandering the family fortune. Conversely, positive landforms outside are signs of virtuous and capable descendants.

- An untimely Facing Star at the Facing palace seeing water could be a sign of excessive greed hurting one's health.

- An untimely Sitting Star at the Sitting palace seeing a mountain could indicate difficulties with childbirth.

- The last 2 points suggest that an "Up Mountain Down Water" chart with untimely Sitting and Facing Stars should not back onto a mountain and face water. This line and others debunked the popular notion that a property with high ground at the back and water in front is always desirable.

Chapter 9
Physical & Emotional Distress

Chapter 9: Physical & Emotional Distress

CHAPTER 9:
Physical & Emotional Distress

SX52: 腹多水而膨脹。

The abdomen bloats with too much water.

"abdomen" = Star-2; "water" = Star-1.

Star-2 (Earth) is supposed to control Star-1(Water), but if Star-2 is untimely and unsupported, it is unable to control the Water, and disintegrates instead.

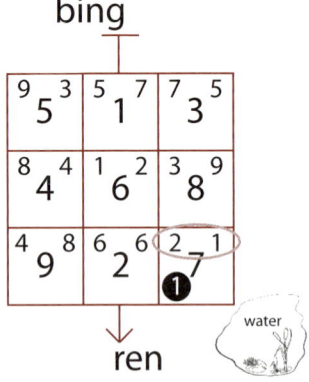

Fig-16: 2-1 combo

Fig-16 illustrates a Period-6 property sitting *bing* facing *ren*. There is a 2-1 Star conjunction at *qian*. Star-2 is out-of-timing in Period-6. Star-1 is grown by *luo shu* Star-6 and Period Star-7 at *qian*. If in addition there is real water outside *qian*, it would be read as a classic case of excessive Water causing Earth to bloat.

The conjunction is not limited to Sitting and Facing Stars. It can be between any 2 Stars resident at the same palace.

The prognosis is stomach or spleen or intestinal disorders.

Chapter 9: Physical & Emotional Distress

SX53: 足以金而蹣跚。

The legs become wobbly on account of metal.

[章作：足見金而蹣跚。

Zhang's version: The legs become wobbly on seeing metal.]

"legs" = Star-3; "metal" = Stars-6, 7.

Star-3 (Wood), if untimely, is severely damaged by Stars-6, 7 (Metal).

A 3-6 or 3-7 Star conjunction provides a sign of fractured limbs (more so 3-6). As Wood element is also associated with the liver, the conjunction could also indicate liver or blood ailments (more so 3-7).

Negative mountain forms outside the affected palace will confirm such a prognosis.

Chapter 9: Physical & Emotional Distress

> **SX54:** 巽宮水路繞乾，爲懸樑之犯。
>
> A waterway or path from *xun* palace looping round to *qian* points to suicide by hanging.
>
> [章作：巽宮水路纏乾，主有吊樑之厄。
>
> Zhang's version: If a waterway or path from *xun* palace loops round to *qian*, the host is in danger of suicide by hanging.]

The Trigram *xun* represents a rope (amongst other things); the Trigram *qian* represents the head.

A rope around the head – what else can it mean?

In Flying Stars terms, the line describes a 4-6 conjunction.

Note that Star-4 on its own at *qian* palace (*luo shu* Star-6) would have yielded a 4-6 conjunction. So would Star-6 at *xun* (luo shu Star-4).

For a prediction to be effective, the Stars must be corroborated by the physical forms. If there is a drain or roadway encircling half the property from Northwest to Southeast or vice-versa, the conditions are fulfilled.

Shen Zu Mian (沈祖綿) and Kong Zhao Su (孔昭蘇), both *xuan kong* heavyweights, commented that this prediction is effective whether the Stars are timely or otherwise.

See sidebar for an anecdote of topical interest.

Chapter 9: Physical & Emotional Distress

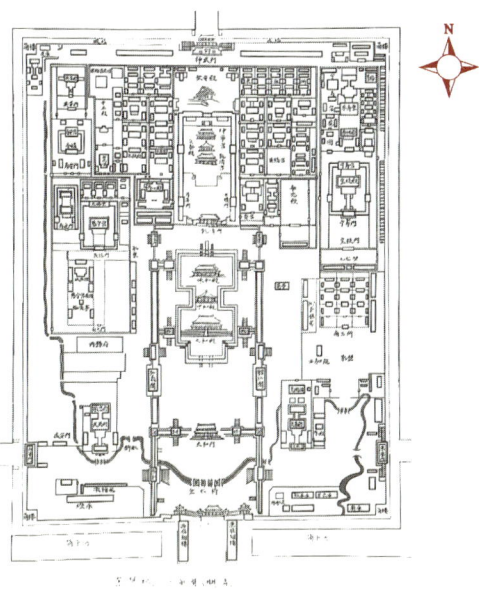

Map of Forbidden City

The Forbidden City in Beijing has this problem. Within the city walls, there is a scenic waterway entering from the Northwest, weaving its way through the West, Southwest and South sectors, and finally exiting at the Southeast corner. See map.

In its history as the Chinese imperial palace for almost 500 years, there was so much frustration and misery within its walls that countless residents, especially neglected concubines and indentured servants, were driven to take their own lives by hanging.

Even an emperor (Chong Zhen 崇禎 of Ming, 1644) hanged himself when the dynasty fell.

To stem the tide, one of the Qing emperors had to issue an imperial edict forbidding any more suicides. Offenders would have their whole families put to death.

Chapter 9: Physical & Emotional Distress

> **SX55:** 兌位明堂破震，主吐血之災。
>
> If water from the "Bright Hall" at *dui* flows out at *zhen*, the host coughs out blood.
>
> [章作：兌位明堂破震，定生吐血之災。
>
> Zhang's version: Water from the "Bright Hall" at *dui* flowing out at *zhen* will surely induce the coughing of blood.]

In this context, "Bright Hall" refers to an area where water collects.

It says that if water originating from *dui* (West) flows out of the compound at *zhen* (East), then it signals illnesses in which the victim coughs out blood.

The Trigram *dui* represents the mouth, blood and the lungs. The Trigram *zhen* represents the liver. *dui* Metal hurts *zhen* Wood – hence blood in the expectorant.

In the language of the Stars: *dui* = Star-7; *zhen* = Star-3.

A 7-3 conjunction at the Facing palace also satisfies the phrase "water from the Bright Hall at *dui* flows out at *zhen*". Of course, the Stars have to be untimely for such misfortune to strike.

Line SX53 also touches on 3-7 Wood-Metal conflict. A 3-7 conjunction is also called "Piercing Heart Killing (穿心煞)". Apart from coughing out blood, it also signifies robbery or punishment at the hands of the law including police brutality, when the Stars are untimely.

Traditionally, Star-3 and Star-7 have unsavory reputations: Star-3 (Rewards Star 祿存星) was reviled for its impulsive and uncouth character, and Star-7 (Broken Soldier Star 破軍星) unloved for its destructive tendencies. But Star-3 also champions aggressiveness and competitive sports; while Star-7 advocates change and communication skills.

In this day and age, where would our sporting heroes be without Star-3? What would happen to our corporate consultants and lawyers without Star-7? Isn't it about time we reevaluate the contributions of these 2 Stars?

[Likewise, Star-8 (Left Assistant Star 左輔星) has traditionally been everyone's darling because of its association with wealth. But then Star-8's wealth comes from mundane hard work. How many millionaires do you know made their fortunes from steadfast employment? Traditional Chinese culture used to discourage radical thinking, but times have changed.]

Chapter 9: Physical & Emotional Distress

SX56: 風行地而硬直難當，室有欺姑之婦。

If the wind blows across the land, hard and unrelenting, the household will have a daughter-in-law that bullies the mother.

"wind" = Star-4 (Wood); "land" = Star-2 (Earth).

A 4-2 conjunction describes a Wood-Earth conflict.

Star-4 represents a woman aged 30-45, and Star-2 the mother. Hence the reading of daughter-in-law bullying the mother is not difficult to visualize.

It goes without saying that the Stars, or at least Star-4, need to be untimely for this to happen.

While "hard and unrelenting" appears to describe the ferocity of the wind, it also alludes to presence of straight and merciless landforms outside the affected palace. In forms *fengshui*, curvy is sentimental while straight is merciless. A mountain range that doesn't twist and turn; a straight road or waterway; a lamppost; etc. are deemed negative features.

As before, Stars and landforms have to back up each other for a prediction to hold true.

Chapter 9: Physical & Emotional Distress

> **SX57:** 火燒天而張牙相鬥，家生罵父之兒。
>
> If fire burns the heavens like opponents baring their teeth at each other, the family will have a child that scolds its father.

"fire" = Star-9 (Fire); "heavens" = Star-6 (Metal).

9-6 describes a Fire-Metal conflict, which is about the most violent of all the elemental conflicts.

Star-6 represents the father, and Star-9 one of his children (2nd daughter). Hence if the Stars are untimely, the conjunction signals the father being rebuked by his child. Under Confucian ethics, scolding one's father is utterly unthinkable.

The phrase "opponents baring their teeth at each other" describes rocky outcrops that appear to snarl at one another. If such negative landforms are present outside the 9-6 palace, then the father-child relationship will be adverse.

Apart from unfilial behaviour, 9-6 also signals injury to the head, meningitis (brain fever), or a stroke.

A 9-6 conjunction at *qian* palace is particularly onerous. It carries the name "Fire Burning Heaven's Gate (火燒天門)". According to Chinese Astronomy, Heaven's Gate is located at the *hai* (亥) sector, and *hai* is part of the Trigram *qian*. A violation signals devastating consequences for the male head of household, or elderly male, or *gua*-6 person.

The reader should be aware that in Period-8, the Period Star-9 resides at *qian*. *qian* itself carries the *luo shu* Star-6. Hence there is already an intrinsic 9-6 conjunction at *qian*. The saving grace is that Star-9 is timely during Period-8. However, if additional Fire Stars visit the palace, or a stove is placed there, excessive Fire could turn it negative, to the detriment of the father.

On the other hand, if Star-6 is timely and there are positive landforms outside, 9-6 could in fact bring good news. Star-9 may be read as the Trigram *li*, within which *bing* (丙) and *ding* (丁) reside. The star charts tell us that the "Heavenly Noble Star (天貴星)" is found at *bing*, and the "Southern Dipper Star (南極星)" at *ding*. These are 2 highly auspicious Stars signifying nobility and long life. Hence under the right conditions, 9-6 could turn out to be highly beneficial to the father. (Line SX75)

Chapter 9 – Summary

- 2-1 with Metal Stars to grow more water plus real water outside indicates stomach, spleen or intestinal disorders.

- 3-6 is a sign of fractured limbs; and 3-7 indicates liver or blood disorders.

- 4-6 backed up by a waterway or road from *xun* looping round to *qian*, or vice versa, is a sign of suicide by hanging.

- 7-3 backed up by water entering from *dui* and exiting *zhen* signals the coughing of blood.

- 7-3 is labelled "Piercing Heart Killing (穿心煞)". Apart from health issues, it signifies robbery or punishment by the law.

- 4-2, backed up by merciless landforms, indicates a daughter-in-law bullying the mother.

- 9-6, backed up by rocky outcrops, indicates a child scolding its father.

- 9-6 at *qian* is called "Fire Burning Heaven's Gate (火燒天門)" and is particularly detrimental to an elderly man or male head of household.

Chapter 10
More the Merrier

CHAPTER 10:
More the Merrier

> **SX58:** 兩局相關，必生雙子。
>
> Two structures taking care of each other will surely produce a pair of sons.
>
> [章作：兩局相關，必生孿子。
>
> Zhang's version: Two structures taking care of each other will surely produce twins.]

The phrase "two structures taking care of each other" is a literal translation but the meaning is ambiguous.

Of the different interpretations put forward, I consider Shen Zu Mian's (沈祖綿) to be the most credible. The line describes a "Prosperous Sitting Prosperous Facing" chart that is supported by 2 or more layers of mountains at the back and 2 or more stages of water collection at the front. In addition, the Sitting and Facing directions must comply with the "Direct/Indirect Spirit" rule (i.e. mountains at Direct Spirit location; water at Indirect Spirit location) in a given Period.

Neither should the bit about producing "pair of sons" or "twins" be taken too literally. It simply alludes to multiple happy events happening simultaneously – could be people and wealth together.

Chapter 10: More the Merrier

> **SX59:** 孤龍單結，定主獨夫。
>
> If the dragon is solitary, the host will surely be lonely.
>
> [章作：孤龍單結，定有獨夫。
>
> Zhang's version: If the dragon is solitary, there will surely be a lonely man.]

The grand daddy of *fengshui* texts, the "Burial Book" did say that a solitary mountain is not a good place for burial because *qi* is only vibrant when the dragons converge, meaning that a solitary mountain has weak *qi*.

The majority of writers interpret Line SX59 to mean that even if the Sitting Star at the Sitting palace is supported by a mountain, people luck (meaning progeny) will still not be good if the mountain is solitary, or if its shape is irregular.

However, there is a dissenting voice which I find notable. It comes from the writer Ke Jian Cheng (柯建成) who argued that Lines SX58 and SX59 should be read together, in form and in substance.

If one takes the position that Line SX58 says that multiple good fortune, in respect of both people and wealth, could befall a property amply supported by both mountains and water, then Line SX59 should imply that if only the Sitting Star is supported, there can only be people luck and not wealth luck, even if the chart is "Prosperous Sitting Prosperous Facing".

Likewise, if there is only water in front and no mountain at the back, then there will only be wealth luck and not people luck.

By extension, "Double Sitting" and "Double Facing" charts would have such issues.

Chapter 10: More the Merrier

Chapter 10 – Summary

- If a "Prosperous Sitting Prosperous Facing" chart is supported by multiple layers of mountains at the back and water in front, then the property is poised to see multiple and simultaneous happy events.

- Even if there is a mountain supporting the Sitting Star at the Sitting palace, people luck may still be deficient if the mountain is solitary or inadequate in other ways.

    Alternatively, if only the Sitting Star is supported but not the Facing Star, then there will only be people luck but not wealth luck.

Chapter 11
Health Issues

CHAPTER 11:
Health Issues

SX60: 坎宮高塞而耳聾。

A high and congested *kan* palace leads to deafness.

The popular interpretation is straightforward. "High and congested" refers to a tight mountainous landscape. Mountain is Earth and *kan* Water – hence elemental conflict. It is further assumed that the timing is Periods-6, 7, 8, 9 when *kan* is Indirect Spirit and therefore should be open and not tight.

Moreover, the Trigram *kan* relates to the ear. The prognosis of deafness is not difficult to visualize.

However, Master Zhang in his annotation hinted that the interpretation should be broadened to treat *kan* as being Star-1 rather than just *kan* palace. Several subsequent writers endorsed that view.

In other words, if Star-1 (Water) is controlled by Star-2 or 5 or 8 (Earth) when it is untimely, and on top of that the external landforms are oppressive, then it signals not only hearing problems but also problems with other bodily functions related to *kan*, as for example: urogenital complaints; constipation; difficulties in conception; miscarriage; blocked arteries; Down syndrome; etc.

Chapter 11: Health Issues

> **SX61:** 離位摧殘而目瞎。
>
> A wrecked *li* location leads to blindness.
>
> [章作：離位傷殘而目瞎。
>
> Zhang's version: A maimed *li* location leads to blindness.]

In the same vein as Line SX60, the superficial interpretation is that as *li gua* relates to sight, a *li* palace that sees unwholesome landforms indicates blindness.

Master Zhang's suggestion to broaden the interpretation also applies here. In fact it applies to all of Lines SX60 to SX63.

In other words, if an untimely Star-9 (Fire) is further aggravated by Star-1 (Water) and/or negative mountain shapes, then any bodily function related to *gua*-9 may be impaired. Issues could include: impaired sight; cardiac problems; scalding; unstable temperaments; etc.

[Interestingly, several texts mentioned that a red coloured building is also considered a Fire Star of sorts, and a negative one to boot. Its presence outside a weakened Star-9 palace is considered detrimental.]

Chapter 11: Health Issues

> **SX62:** 兌缺陷而唇亡齒寒。
>
> A flawed *dui* palace leads to "the lips' demise exposing the teeth to bitter cold" (idiom, see sidebar).

Superficially, as *dui gua* relates to the mouth, seriously flawed landforms outside *dui* palace could indicate mouth related problems like a cleft lip exposing the teeth.

More broadly, *dui* is synonymous with Star-7. When Star-7 (Metal) is out-of-timing and is further aggravated by Star-9 (Fire) and/or negative landforms, then body parts and functions related to Star-7 could be at risk. A cleft lip is only an example.

Other problems could include: toothache; cough; throat infections; speech impediments; lung infections; menstrual issues; sexually transmitted diseases; wounded by a knife; etc.

As Star-7 represents "Early Heaven Fire", and Star-9 represents "Later Heaven Fire", a conjunction of these 2 Stars indicates enhanced fire risks, when the Stars are untimely. This aspect is discussed extensively in the "Purple White Script" Lower Scroll.

The phrase "the lips' demise exposing the teeth to bitter cold (唇亡齒寒)" is in fact a well known idiom, but for some strange reason, the idiomatic meaning is ignored and the literal meaning adopted instead in this case. In Chinese literary tradition, this is a rare occurrence indeed. Looks like the author Wu Jing Luan (吳景鸞) was playing a trick on his readers.

For literary interest, the idiom is

"The lips' demise exposing the teeth to bitter cold":

This proverb originated from the Spring & Autumn Period of Chinese history (770~476 BCE). The Duchy of Jin (晉), one of the larger states, wanted to attack a small neighbour called the Duchy of Guo (虢). To get to Guo, Jin's army had to pass through another small territory called the Duchy of Lu (虞).

So the Duke of Jin asked for the Duke of Lu's cooperation and offered him gifts of precious jade and sleek horses. One of Lu's advisers by the name of Gong Zhi Qi (宮之奇) promptly cautioned the Duke, saying that Lu and Guo were two small states that depended on each other like the lips and the teeth. If the lips ceased to exist, the teeth could not survive the cold.

But the Duke of Lu was tempted and agreed to help Jin against Guo. In due course Jin conquered Guo, and on the return journey swallowed up Lu as well. The jade and horses went back to Jin.

The proverb is used to describe two interdependent parties that will survive or perish together.

Chapter 11: Health Issues

explained in the sidebar.

> **SX63:** 艮傷殘而筋枯臂折。
>
> A maimed *gen* palace leads to withered ligaments and fractured arm.
>
> [章作：艮破碎而筋枯臂折。
>
> A crumbling *gen* palace leads to withered ligaments and fractured arm.]

Superficially, as the Trigram *gen* relates to the backbone and limbs, negative landforms outside *gen* palace could indicate fractured limbs and other orthopedic problems.

More broadly, *gen* is represented by Star-8. When Star-8 (Earth) is out-of-timing and attacked by Stars-3, 4 (Wood), and further aggravated by adverse landforms, body parts and functions associated with Star-8 stand to be impacted negatively.

Problems could include: fractured limbs; locomotive disorders; rheumatoid arthritis; neurological disorders; etc.

As the Trigram *gen* and Star-8 also represent young children, a weak Star-8 under attack could also indicate children getting hurt.

Chapter 11: Health Issues

> **SX64:** 山地被風，還生瘋疾。
>
> When mountain and earth are swept by wind, mental illness ensues.
>
> [章作：山地被風吹，還生風疾。
>
> Zhang's version: When mountain and earth are swept by wind, rheumatism ensues.]

"mountain" = Star-8; "earth" = Star-2; "wind" = Star-4.

8-4 or 2-4 represents an Earth-Wood elemental clash. If Star-8 or Star-2 is out-of-timing, and further aggravated by negative landforms, then a negative prognosis is to be expected.

The popular version says "mental illness (瘋疾)", whereas Zhang's version says "rheumatism (風疾)". The 2 ailments appear to be worlds apart, but the 2 terms are phonetically identical. Moreover, mental instability was thought to be caused by wind in the head at one time. So both versions are equally valid.

Rheumatism is only one possible outcome. The other problems associated with Star-8 under attack are mentioned under Line-SX63.

The problems arising from Star-2 being mauled are: abdominal disorders including stomach/spleen/pancreas; digestive system dysfunctions; muscular pains; skin disease; gynecological issues; etc.

Star-2 also represents the ultimate *yin*. Hence Star-2 in trouble could also precipitate depression, hallucination, apparitions, haunting, and the like.

Chapter 11: Health Issues

> **SX65:** 雷風金伐，定被刀傷。
>
> When thunder and wind are attacked by metal, being wounded by a knife is unavoidable.
>
> [章作：雷風因金死，定被刀兵。
>
> When the death of thunder and wind is caused by metal, injury in battle is unavoidable.]

"thunder" = Star-3 (Wood); "wind" = Star-4 (Wood); "metal" = Stars-6, 7 (Metal).

The topic of Wood-Metal conflict has been discussed several times in this text. This line merely adds to that discussion, this time focusing on the effects on the human body.

The allegory between Wood being cut by Metal and the body being wounded by a metal object is obvious, but the Wood Stars also represent other body parts:

Star-3: liver, gall bladder, legs, fingers, hair, body hair, nerves, etc.

Star-4: liver, buttocks, breasts, nerves, respiratory system, alimentary canal, intestines, left side of the body in general, etc.

The effect of Wood Stars punished by Metal Stars and negative landforms may be manifested in the form of ailments affecting any of these body parts.

As to what is the difference between 3-6, 4-6, 3-7 and 4-7? Let's think of Star-6 as an axe and Star-7 as a pocketknife. Similarly, Star-3 may be likened to a tree and Star-4 to herbaceous plants. Evidently an axe is more effective at felling a tree (3-6) than trimming the grass (4-6); just as a pocketknife will do a better job picking flowers (4-7) than trying to cut down a tree (3-7).

Chapter 11: Health Issues

Chapter 11 – Summary

- *kan* palace or Star-1 under attack indicates hearing problems; urogenital complaints; constipation; difficulties in conception; miscarriage; blocked arteries; Down syndrome; etc.

- A distressed *li* palace or Star-9 signals blindness; cardiac problems; scalding; unstable temperaments; etc.

- *dui* palace or Star-7 under attack denotes a cleft lip; toothache; cough; throat infections; speech impediments; lung infections; menstrual issues; STD; wounded by a knife; etc.

- A maimed *gen* palace or Star-8 hints at fractured limbs; locomotive disorders; rheumatoid arthritis; neurological disorders; young children getting hurt; etc.

- 8-4, 2-4 tell of rheumatism or mental illness. The ailments associated with Star-8 and Star-2 also apply.

  Star-2 is related to the abdomen, muscles, skin and the female reproductive organs. Star-2 also stands for the ultimate *yin*. Hence a troubled Star-2 could also be a sign of depression, hallucination, apparitions, haunting, and the like.

- 3-6, 4-6, 3-7, 4-7: Wood cut by Meal. Being wounded by a knife is a natural. Besides that, Star-3 relates to the legs, hair, etc; whereas Star-4 relates to the buttocks, breasts, respiratory system, alimentary canal, intestines, etc. Both Wood Stars are associated with the liver and the nervous system.

Chapter 12
Of Minors & Seniors

CHAPTER 12:
Of Minors & Seniors

SX66: 家有少亡，只爲沖殘子息卦。

If there is death of a minor in the family, it's only because the children Trigrams are damaged in a clash.

SX67: 庭無耆耄，多因栽破父母爻。

If there is an absence of old folks in a household, it's largely because the parent Trigram lines are severed.

[章作：庭無耆老，都因攻破父母爻。

Zhang's version: Marginally different words but the same meaning.]

Lines SX66 & SX67 should be read together.

The terms "children Trigrams" and "parent Trigrams" are not clearly defined. Different writers interpreted them differently. Master Zhang's annotation on these 2 lines is nebulous, to say the least.

Taking the 8 Trigrams as a whole, *qian* and *kun* represent the parents, and the other 6 Trigrams the children. That is only the macro view.

Within each of the 8 Trigrams, the complete Trigram can be regarded as a parent, and the 3 individual lines of the Trigram its children. This is the micro view.

There is a third interpretation: the prosperous Star of the Period (say, Star-8 in Period-8) represents the parents, and the future prosperous Stars (Stars-9, 1 in Period-8) represent the children and grandchildren.

The words "Trigram (卦)" and "Trigram lines (爻)" are used, in a poetic way,

Chapter 12: Of Minors & Seniors

to denote a palace or a Star.

Are these definitions adequate to explain Lines SX65 & SX66? I think not.

Kong Zhao Su (孔昭蘇) and Zhong Yi Ming (鐘義明) are more forthright. In their explanations, the current prosperous Sitting Star (for example, Sitting Star-8 in Period-8) is taken as the point of reference.

If the prosperous Sitting Star lands at the Facing palace, as in a "Down Water" chart, and the landforms outside do not support it (for example vast expanse of water), then people matters are likely to suffer, meaning sickness, lack of descendants, even death in the family.

Even if the prosperous Sitting Star lands at the Sitting palace, as in a "Prosperous Sitting" chart, the same negative deduction is made if the external landforms are not supportive (for example water or deformed mountain shapes).

Take the case of a Period-8 property sitting *kun* facing *gen* (Fig-17): it is an "Up Mountain Down Water" chart. If Sitting Star-8 at the Facing palace sees flat land and water without any "Table Mountain" to give it even minimal support, then people luck is likely to be bad. A jargon term used to describe this scenario is "mountain dragon descends to the water (山龍下水)", sometimes abbreviated to just "Down Water (下水)".

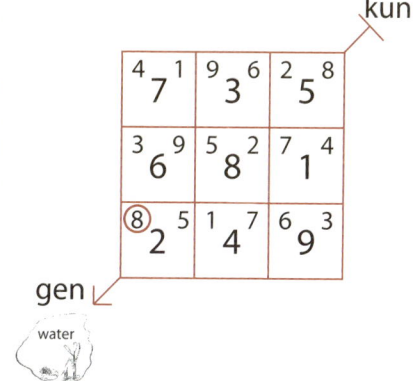

Fig-17: prosperous Sitting Star compromised

Now comes the question of who in the family is most likely to be impacted:

If the unsupportive landform outside the Facing palace extends over the whole of the Trigram, i.e. 3 contiguous Mountains on the 24-Mountains Plate, then it is the parents who stand to be impacted. The absence of old folks in a household could be attributed to that (Line SX66).

Chapter 12: Of Minors & Seniors

On the other hand, if the unfavorable landform covers only 1 or 2 of the Mountains within a Trigram, and not the whole Trigram (palace), then the children or grandchildren are likely to be impacted (Line SX65). If the afflicted Mountain is *yang*, it indicates a male child; if the Mountain is *yin*, a female.

An alternative, and equally valid, interpretation would be that if the unfavorable landforms are outside the palaces having the future prosperous Sitting Stars (Star-9 at *li*, Star-1 at *kan* in Fig-17), then the children or grandchildren are impacted. The same concept is invoked in Line SX08 earlier.

Do note that the 2 lines are written in a rather tentative way: if there is a death, it is because... etc. The lines do not say that the unfavorable landforms will cause death. There is a subtle but significant difference. Surely it would be unrealistic and irresponsible to predict death just because the landforms are unfavorable. At least the old text did not exaggerate this time ☺

Chapter 12: Of Minors & Seniors

Chapter 12 – Summary

- A negative landform outside the palace in which the prosperous Sitting Star resides denotes adverse people luck, and in the worst case, even death. But who will be the victim?

- If the negative landform extends over all 3 Mountains of the *luo pan* within that palace, then the parents are targeted; but if the negative landform only covers 1 or 2 of the Mountains, then the children will be the victims: *yang* Mountain – male child; *yin* Mountain – female child.

- Alternatively, a negative landform outside the palaces having the future prosperous Sitting Stars will also impact the children's wellbeing.

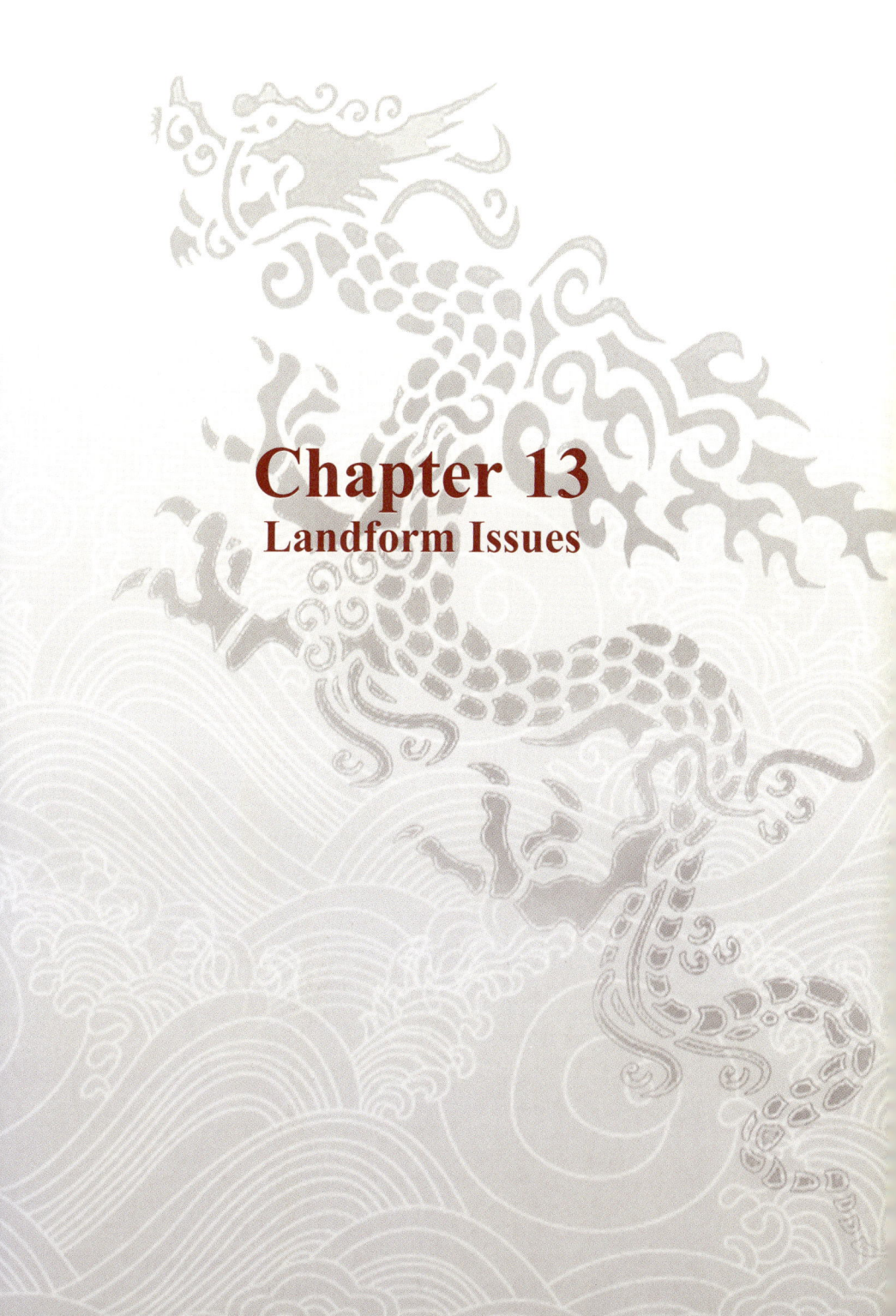

Chapter 13
Landform Issues

CHAPTER 13:
Landform Issues

SX68: 漏道在坎宮，遺精洩血。

A leakage path at *kan* palace signals unconscious seminal discharge and bleeding.

"Leakage path" is a literal translation of the Chinese text. Master Zhang explained that term should refer to a 2-way split in the outgoing waterway, not just any drain.

kan represents the kidneys, urinary system and reproductive organs. Hence any irregular outflow at *kan* palace would indicate renal or urogenital disorders that could result in seminal discharge or bleeding.

Chapter 13: Landform Issues

SX69: 破軍居巽位，顛疾風狂。

Broken Soldier residing at *xun* location signals mental disorders.

"Broken Soldier" can refer to Star-7, or to a mountain of a particular shape belonging to the Metal group. [In landform *fengshui*, a "Broken Soldier" mountain has massive descending ridges that look like octopus tentacles. The mountain is usually rocky and hardly good looking.]

If we read Line SX69 as a response to Line SX68 (the 2 lines being a couplet), then "Broken Soldier" should be interpreted as an ugly mountain. In other words, an unwholesome mountain at *xun* palace could cause mental disorders.

Why mental disorders? Well, the Trigram *xun* represents wind. In the old days, madness or eccentricity was thought to be due to wind in the head.

Some writers take the view that "Broken Soldier residing at *xun*…" refers to a 7-4 conjunction. A Metal-Wood elemental clash is inherent. If the Stars are untimely and are further aggravated by negative landforms, then mental instability, wanton behaviour in women (considered a mental aberration in the old days), lesbian tendencies, and other disruptions to the social order could result.

This explanation, however, lacks a parallel in Line SX68 to lend it support.

Chapter 13: Landform Issues

> **SX70:** 開口筆插離方，必落孫山之外。
>
> A frayed brush inserted at *li* location indicates certain failure in the exams.

The Trigram *li* stands for brilliance and cultured behaviour. If a narrow and tall mountain with a pointed tip is seen outside *li* palace, it indicates outstanding scholarship. That is provided the pointed tip is wholesome and elegant. Such a mountain shape is called a "Scholar's Brush (文筆山)"

If, on the other hand, the mountain top is split into two or more peaks, it will look like a worn (frayed) brush that cannot be used for calligraphy. The brilliance of *li* dims, and one's hopes at the exams are dashed.

The Chinese text invokes an idiom "to fall outside of Sun Shan (名落孫山)" to describe failure at the exams. There is a rather curious story behind it. I thought I'd relate the story for literary interest. See sidebar.

> *There was a Song Dynasty scholar by the name of Sun Shan (孫山) who was noted for his sense of humour.*
>
> *Sun sat for the provincial level civil service exam, together with a fellow candidate from the same village. Sun managed to scrape through and his name was posted last on the pass list. The other fellow failed.*
>
> *When Sun returned to his village ahead of the other fellow, the latter's folks naturally enquired how their son fared. Sun was embarrassed to tell them straight, so he made up the following prose:*
>
> *"Sun Shan was at the end of the pass list. Your virtuous son fell outside of Sun Shan. (解名盡處是孫山，賢郎更在孫山外。)"*
>
> *We would never know whether his listeners got the message, but the phrase "to fall outside of Shun Shan" became an idiom meaning failure at an exam.*

Chapter 13: Landform Issues

> **SX71:** 離鄉砂見艮位，定遭驛路之亡。
>
> A "Departing Embrace" (landform *fengshui* term) at *gen* location indicates inevitable death away from home.
>
> [章作：離鄉砂飛艮位，定亡驛路之中。
>
> A "Departing Embrace" flying off at *gen* location indicates inevitable death in the course of one's travels.]

An "Embrace" is a landform *fengshui* term for a hill chain, or the wing of a hill, that extends round the left or right side, or the front of the subject property. It protects the subject property and prevents the *qi* from leaking away. A "Departing Embrace", also called "Reverse Embrace", is one such hill that curves away from the subject property, thereby defeating its protective function. It is considered a negative landform.

The *gen* Trigram represents a mountain, also a narrow mountainous path. Yet another interpretation of *gen* is to stop [from the *yi jing* (易經) treatise "Speaking of Hexagrams (說卦傳)"].

If a hill turns away at *gen* palace, it means that what should stop doesn't stop, or a mountain fails to curtail movement. Clearly a bad omen.

To die away from home was considered a terrible curse in the old days.

As *gen* is synonymous with Star-8, this negative prognosis only applies when Star-8 is out-of-timing.

> *"Speaking of Hexagrams (說卦傳)" is an important treatise dating back to the Qin Dynasty (221~207 BCE). It is one of the early documents setting out to explain the "yi jing (易經)".*
>
> *Of the 8 Trigrams, it has this to say:*
>
> *qian is to be strong 乾健也 (Star-6)*
> *kun is to comply 坤順也 (Star-2)*
> *zhen is to move 震動也 (Star-3)*
> *xun is to enter 巽入也 (Star-4)*
> *kan is to sink 坎陷也 (Star-1)*
> *li is to be beautiful 離麗也 (Star-9)*
> *gen is to stop 艮止也 (Star-8)*
> *dui is to speak 兌說也 (Star-7)*
>
> *These attributes of the Trigrams, and by extension the Stars, are often called up to explain certain Star conjunctions.*

Chapter 13: Landform Issues

Chapter 13 – Summary

➢ A split in the outgoing waterway at *kan* denotes renal or urogenital disorders that could result in bleeding or seminal discharge.

➢ An ugly mountain at *xun* speaks of mental disorders.

➢ A narrow based tall mountain with multiple peaks seen at *li* is a sign of failure in an exam.

➢ A "Departing Embrace" at *gen* warns of death away from home.

Chapter 14
More Conjunctions, Good & Bad

CHAPTER 14:
More Conjunctions, Good & Bad

SX72: 金水多情，貪花戀酒。

Metal and Water are flirtatious, implying addiction to merrymaking and alcohol.

"Metal" refers to Star-7, a young girl, a fun loving female. It cannot be Star-6 in this case as an old man is not supposed to be flirtatious ☹

"Water" refers to Star-1, a young adult male, and liquid refreshments ☺

That makes 7-1 a potentially scandalous mixture! But only when the Stars are untimely.

Usually Star-7 calls the shots. Star-1 being a "White Star" (Stars-1, 6, 8 are the "White Stars") has a mild character, timely or otherwise. Incapacitated and frustrated maybe when out-or-timing, but never belligerent. Just as in a young woman/older man relationship, guess who's usually the demanding party?

Chapter 14: More Conjunctions, Good & Bad

> **SX73:** 木金相反，背義忘恩。
>
> Wood and Metal transposed implies betrayal and ingratitude.

"Wood" here refers to Stars-3, 4; "Metal" to Stars-6, 7. The pairs discussed here are 3,7 and 4-6.

The discussion usually centres on 3-7, as a knife carving up a tree trunk is conceivably more excruciating than an axe trying to cut grass. Moreover, Star-6 is a "White Star" (see previous line).

The conjunction 3-7 has been discussed elsewhere in this book. It is called "Piercing Heart Killing (穿心煞)". The name says it all. Of course, for the negative attributes to surface, the Stars must be out-of-timing, and/or aggravated by negative landforms.

The word "transposed" describes several scenarios:

– If Star-7 resides at *zhen* and Star-3 at *dui*, the Stars are in the wrong palaces. This is a transposition of locations, also called "Inverse Siren" (see Appendix-1);

– If the external landforms are the opposite of what one would like to see, it is a transposition of landforms. For example, prosperous Sitting Star at the Sitting palace sees water and prosperous Facing Star at the Facing palace sees mountain;

– If a Star is adequately supported by external landforms, but is out-of-timing, it can be said to be a transposition of time.

– Mountains that turn away and rivers that crash out are also called "transposed", according to some writers, but I think that's stretching it.

In terms of character traits, Metal stands for righteousness, just as Wood stands for benevolence. Hence beleaguered Metal implies betrayal, just as beleaguered Wood implies ingratitude.

Chapter 14: More Conjunctions, Good & Bad

SX74: 震庚會局，文臣而兼武將之權。

zhen meeting with *geng* indicates that a civil officer will also hold military power.

"*zhen*" (Star-3) encompasses 3 Mountains: *jia, mao, yi*; whereas "*geng*" on the other hand is only one out of 3 Mountains under *dui* (Star-7). Hence the pairing of *zhen* with *geng* appears incongruent.

Some writers, including Master Zhang in his annotation, singled out *jia* within *zhen*, but their explanations are rather forced. Other writers simply took *zhen* to mean Star-3, and *geng* to mean Star-7.

In previous discussions of 3-7, the conjunction was always viewed negatively ("Piercing Heart Killing", etc). This time round, 3-7 turns positive. The difference is in the timeliness of the Stars.

But why "civil officer also holds military power"?

Zhang explained it in terms of the heavenly stars, which are real stars observed by the ancient astronomers. The *luo pan* is also used to demarcate the sky into 24 segments (aka 24-Mountains). The star "Heavenly Wealth (天祿)" is found at *mao* within *zhen*. This star is associated with high ranking civil positions. Similarly the star "Military Baron (武爵)" is found at *geng*. Hence the conjunction of these 2 stars represents simultaneous civil and military power. So said Master Zhang, but this explanation is by no means unanimously accepted among the writers.

In modern society, it could translate to outstanding performance in both academic pursuits and sports.

Kong Zhao Su (孔昭蘇) cited the example of a Period-3 property sitting *you* facing *mao* (Fig-18). The conjunction 7-3 occurs at the Facing palace, and in addition Sitting Star-3 resides at the Sitting palace (with *luo shu* Star-7). Star-

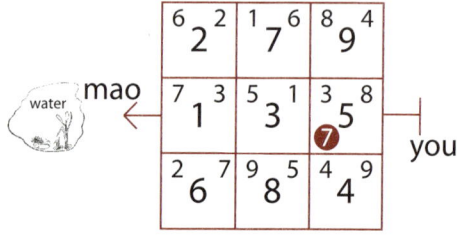

Fig-18: civil & military power

3 is prosperous. Kong commented that if there is water outside the Facing palace, then the positive prognosis would be fulfilled.

I am not altogether convinced, as water at *zhen* in Period-3 would have violated the Direct/Indirect Spirit rule. Moreover Star-3 at *zhen* is a Hidden Siren. Nonetheless, the example is worth studying.

Chapter 14: More Conjunctions, Good & Bad

SX75: 丁丙朝乾，貴客而有耆耋之壽。

ding or *bing* facing *qian* represents persons of high status and long life.

"*ding*" and "*bing*" are 2 Mountains within *li* palace (Star-9); and "*qian*" is plainly Star-6. If the line refers to a 9-6 conjunction, why only *ding* and *bing*, and not *wu* (午)?

Here again, Master Zhang in his annotation resorted to the heavenly stars: the "South Polar Star (南極星)" residing at *ding* represents longevity; and the star "Greater Covert (太微)" residing at *bing* is associated with status (equivalent to the Inner Cabinet). Hence, together they stand for high status and long life.

As to why *ding* and *bing* but not *wu*: speculation is that *wu* has too much Fire in it, thereby raising the spectre of 9-6 "Fire Burning Heaven's Gate" (Line SX57).

The difference between this line and Line SX57 is of course the timeliness of the Stars and the support provided by the external landforms.

Strictly speaking, the supportive mountain should be located at *ding* or *bing* rather than *wu*, and it goes without saying that the mountain shape must be elegant.

The 6 lines from SX74 to SX79 describe the positive outcomes of certain Star conjunctions when the Stars are timely and supported. This is a welcome change from the prophesies of doom elsewhere in the text.

Chapter 14: More Conjunctions, Good & Bad

> **SX76:** 天市合丙坤，富堪敵國。
>
> When "Heavenly City" combines with *bing* and *kun*, one's wealth will be able to challenge the country's.

The "Heavenly City Constellation (天市垣)" is located at *gen*, and therefore refers to Star-8. "*bing*" = Star-9; "*kun*" = Star-2.

Line SX76 says that is a meeting of the Stars-8, 9, 2 indicates fabulous wealth that's comparable to the national coffers. Is that an exaggeration? Not quite. There is no shortage of examples in history when a country went bankrupt and had to turn to rich merchants for a bailout, and this did not happen only in China.

The Heavenly City Constellation is associated with wealth, especially wealth generated by commerce. The Fire of Star-9 grows the Earth of Star-8. Star-2 forms a Later Heaven combination (combo-10) with Star-8. Both 8 and 2 are wealth Stars when timely.

Hence in the Lower Cycle when Stars-8 & 9 are timely, and Star-2 is not that weak (explained in "Purple White Script" Line PW112), the appearance of these 3 Stars at a palace, supported by favorable water outside, signals the accumulation of great wealth.

Chapter 14: More Conjunctions, Good & Bad

SX77: 離壬會子癸，喜產多男。

When *li, ren* meets with *zi, gui*, chances are more boys (than girls) will be born.

"*li*" = Star-9. "*ren*", "*zi*" and "*gui*" make up the Trigram "*kan*" = Star-1.

From the family relationship perspective, Star-9 represents the middle daughter and Star-1 the middle son. Hence 9-1 is deemed a natural and proper pair (正配). Star-9 is also a sign of happy events. From the Hexagram viewpoint, 9-1 produces the "Accomplished (水火既濟)" Hexagram.

All these point to the consummate outcome of a marriage, or more crudely, a successful mating exercise.

Needless to say, the Stars must be timely and well supported.

As to why more boys than girls, no one has offered a satisfactory explanation. In fact Shen Zu Mian (沈祖綿) did say this line is about the hardest to explain in the whole text.

Let me try: in the old days, the primary purpose of a marriage was to produce a male heir to carry on the family name. Hence only the birth of a son, and not a daughter, was considered a real accomplishment. In other words, the output of a 9-1 conjunction under the right conditions should be a male child. [I know this explanation will hardly be acceptable to women's rights advocates ☹]

Chapter 14: More Conjunctions, Good & Bad

> **SX78:** 四生有合人文旺。
>
> If there are combinations within the "4 Growths", humanity thrives.

Of the 12 Earthly Branches, *yin* (寅), *shen* (申), *si* (巳), *hai* (亥) are known as the "4 Growths (四生)". In terms of Flying Stars, they are Stars-8, 2, 4, 6 respectively.

By the "Earthly Branches 6-Combo (地支六合)" formula, *yin* combines with *hai* (8-6); *si* combines with *shen* (4-2).

8-6 is an Earth-Metal growth relationship. Although 4-2 is nominally a Wood-Earth clash, such a clash is not destructive, as it is *yi* Wood (herbaceous plants) clinging onto *ji* Earth (soft earth). The relationship is in fact symbiotic: Earth anchors the Wood, and Wood holds the Earth together.

Moreover, Line SX78 presupposes that the Stars are timely and supported. As human values are involved, mountain support is implied rather than water.

Chapter 14: More Conjunctions, Good & Bad

SX79: 四旺無沖田宅饒。

> If there are no clashes within the 4 "Prosperous", property prospers.

This line follows-on from Line SX78.

The Earthly Branches *zi* (子), *wu* (午), *mao* (卯), *you* (酉) are called the "4 Prosperous (四旺)". The corresponding Flying Stars are Stars-1, 9, 3, 7 respectively.

1-9, 3-7 and 9-7 are clashes. "No clashes" means these conjunctions are excluded. That leaves 1-3, 3-9 and 7-1. All 3 are growth relationships.

If the Stars are timely and supported by water at the right places, property wealth grows.

Actually, Lines SX78 and SX79 may be read together to mean that the Star conjunctions 8-6, 4-2, 1-3, 3-9 and 7-1 are highly beneficial when timely. If supported by mountains, then humanity thrives; if supported by water, then wealth.

Chapter 14: More Conjunctions, Good & Bad

Chapter 14 – Summary

- 7-1 means flirtations and drink, an enjoyable but risky mix.
- 3-7 when weak warns of betrayal and ingratitude.
- 3-7 when strong envisions combined civil and military authority, or excellence in both academic pursuits and sports.
- 9-6 when strong bestows high status and long life.
- 8-9-2 signifies fabulous wealth comparable to the national coffers.
- 9-1 portends a successful marriage and birth of an heir.
- 8-6, 4-2 facilitate the development of humanity and human values.
- 1-3, 3-9, 7-1 enhance property wealth.

Chapter 15
Incapacitated, Out of Place

Chapter 15: Incapacitated, Out of Place

CHAPTER 15:
Incapacitated, Out of Place

SX80: 丑未換局，而出僧尼。
A change in *chou-wei* structure will produce monks and nuns.

"*chou*" = Star-8; "*wei*" = Star-2.

"Change in structure" is an oblique way of saying that an otherwise good chart is incapacitated for some reason or other.

An incapacitated Star-8 characterizes a lonely man, just as an incapacitated Star-2 symbolizes widowhood or a woman detached from society – hence the suggestion of monks and nuns.

Take for example the case of a Period-8 property sitting *wei* facing *chou* (Fig-19). This is a "Prosperous Sitting Prosperous Facing" chart. A 2-8 conjunction resides at the Facing palace; and at the Sitting palace, Sitting Star-8 combines with *luo shu* Star-2. By right the chart should enable both people and wealth luck.

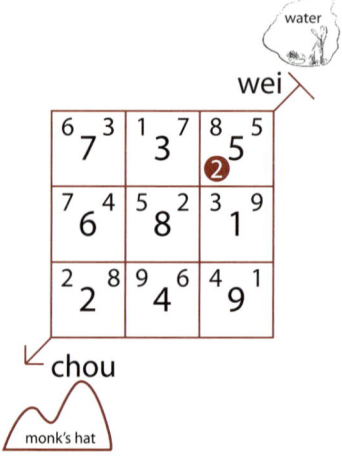

Fig-19: 8-2 incapacitated

132 Secrets of Xuan Kong

Chapter 15: Incapacitated, Out of Place

However, if the required landforms are reversed, i.e. mountain in front and water behind, then the chart is incapacitated, or in Line SX80's language, a change in structure has occurred. People luck turns bad, producing lonely people or people withdrawn from society.

The text mentions monks and nuns. Now monkhood is not bad per se, but from the mainstream social perspective, these people have turned their backs on society, and their vows of celibacy are counter-productive (pun intended ☺).

From another perspective, monks and nuns answer, or are supposed to answer, a call to spirituality. That's not a bad thing. For 8-2 to produce spiritual persons, the landforms often provide some signs. Certain mountain shapes are associated with spirituality, one of which is the "Monk's Hat (僧帽)" illustrated in Fig-19. If such a mountain is seen at *chen, xu, chou* or *wei* (the 4 "Graveyards"), one can expect spiritually inclined persons to be born or congregate at that locality.

Chapter 15: Incapacitated, Out of Place

> **SX81:** 震巽失宮，而生賊丐。
>
> *zhen* and *xun* losing their palaces will produce thieves and vagrants.

"*zhen*" = Star-3; "*xun*" = Star-4.

"Losing their palaces" means the Stars are not where they ought to be, i.e. out of place. It may help visualization to think of the Wood Stars as plants. Plants in general do not like to be uprooted and relocated. The displacement could be unsettling or worse.

Taking a broader view, the 2 expressions: "losing their palaces" herein, and "change in structure" in the previous line, both suggest that potentially beneficial Stars or Star conjunctions are being wasted, as in the case of "Up Mountain Down Water" charts, untimely Stars, or negative landforms.

An unwholesome Star-3 represents thieves and robbers; whilst Star-4 under duress brings about instability and dishonesty – hence the words "thieves and vagrants". In modern society, that would relate to robberies, frauds and scams.

A 3-4 conjunction, when untimely or threatened, suggests deception, fraud, embezzlement, manipulation by a female, an affair in which the man comes off badly; etc.

The following example (Fig-20) is cited by Shen Zu Mian (沈祖綿), Kong Zhao Su (孔昭蘇), and others. Let's examine it: Period-4 property sitting *you* facing *mao*, "Up Mountain Down Water" chart. That's bad enough, but the presence of Sitting Star-4 at *zhen* compounds the problem.

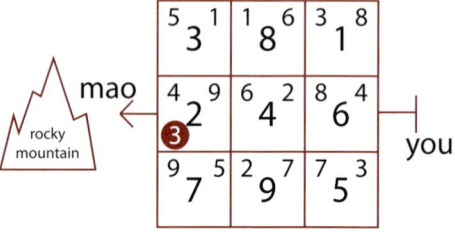

Fig-20: 3-4

As before, any such prediction should be corroborated by the external landforms.

Chapter 15: Incapacitated, Out of Place

Chapter 15 – Summary

➢ An impaired Sitting Star-8 is the sign of a man dissociated from society at large, such as a monk. If Star-2, then a woman in a comparable situation.

➢ A distressed Star-3 is personified by a thief, and Star-4 a vagrant. 3-4 when untimely suggests manipulation, deception, fraud, embezzlement, etc.

Chapter 16
Special P5 Charts

CHAPTER 16:
Special P5 Charts

> **SX82:** 南離北坎，位極中央。
>
> Southern *li* and Northern *kan*, the location is right at the centre.
>
> [章作：南離北坎，位極中天。
>
> Zhang's version: marginally different wording but same meaning.]

"Southern *li*" = Star-9; "Northern *kan*" = Star-1.

Taken at face value, the line simply says there is a 9-1 conjunction at the central palace. That can only happen with Period-5 North/South facing properties – altogether 4 charts.

What then? The line doesn't say.

Of these 4 charts, 2 are "Prosperous Sitting Prosperous Facing". These are special charts that will foster exceptionally good fortune in both people and wealth matters, if supported by external landforms of course. These charts are shown in Fig-21.

In the left-hand chart (sitting *zi* or *gui*, facing *wu* or *ding*), the Sitting Star-5 at *kan* may be replaced by 1, and the Facing Star-5 at *li* replaced by 9. So we have Sitting Star-1 at the Sitting palace and Facing Star-9 at the Facing palace, i.e. the Sitting and Facing Stars at the central palace have moved to the Sitting and Facing palaces respectively.

Chapter 16: Special P5 Charts

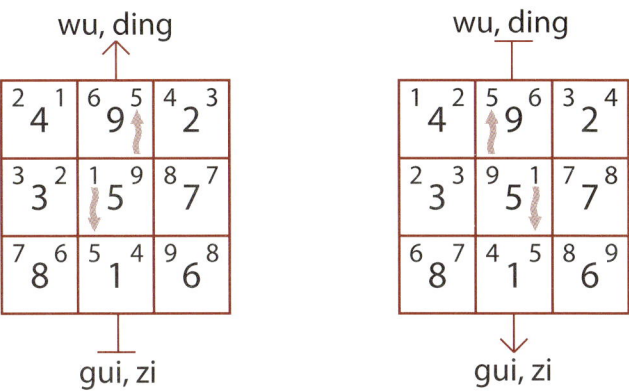

Fig-21: 1-9 at central palace

In the right-hand chart (sitting *wu* or *ding*, facing *zi* or *gui*), the Sitting Star-5 at *li* may be replaced by 9, and the Facing Star-5 at *kan* replaced by 1. So we have Sitting Star-9 at the Sitting palace and Facing Star-1 at the Facing palace, i.e. the relevant Stars at the central palace have moved to the Sitting and Facing palaces.

[The replacement of Star-5 with another Star residing at the central palace is a lesser known *xuan kong* manoeuvre. The rationale is that Star-5 has no Trigram of its own; it therefore 'floats' and is able to take on the personality of another Star when there is reason to do so.]

The other 2 charts are "Up Mountain Down Water". They are not of the same league.

Secrets of Xuan Kong

Chapter 16: Special P5 Charts

> **SX83:** 長庚啓明，交戰四國。
>
> "Long *geng*" and "Messenger of Brightness" indicate fighting battles in 4 countries.

"Long *geng* (長庚)" and "Messenger of Brightness (啓明)" are both aliases of the planet Venus. If the planet is seen in the Western skies, it is called "Long *geng*"; if it appears in the East, it is called "Messenger of Brightness" (see sidebar).

In other words, "Long *geng*" = Star-7; "Messenger of Brightness" = Star-3.

So once again we are back to 3-7. This conjunction is discussed in no less than 8 lines of this text. If the "Purple White Script" is said to be obsessed with 4-1, the "Secrets of *xuan kong*" is no less obsessed with 3-7!

Taking the cue from Line SX82 above, we are now looking for 3-7 at the central palace. This only happens with Period-5 East/West facing properties.

By the same argument as in Line SX82, the 2 charts shown in Fig-22 will have the Sitting Star and Facing Star at the central palace migrating to the Sitting palace and Facing palace, respectively. This again makes them rather special charts.

> *In Chinese astronomy, the planet Venus is usually called the "Great White Metal Star (太白金星)", but it carries several aliases.*
>
> *As the orbit of Venus is relatively close to the Sun, the planet is only visible either just before dawn in the Eastern skies, or at dusk in the Western skies.*
>
> *If seen at dawn, it is called "Messenger of Brightness (啓明)", and at dusk it is called "Long geng (長庚)"*
>
> *Venus may well be a goddess of love in Greek mythology, but to the Chinese, it is a Metal star and is therefore more inclined to aggression than love, although some predatory females will tell you it's the same thing* ☺

"Fighting battles in 4 countries" describes a victorious commander leading military campaigns to all 4 quadrants of the map. These special charts, if properly supported, are capable of producing great generals. As to whether war is good or bad, it depends on the reference viewpoint. To a military commander, war represents an opportunity for glory and promotion, never mind the agony it inflicts on the populace ☹

Chapter 16: Special P5 Charts

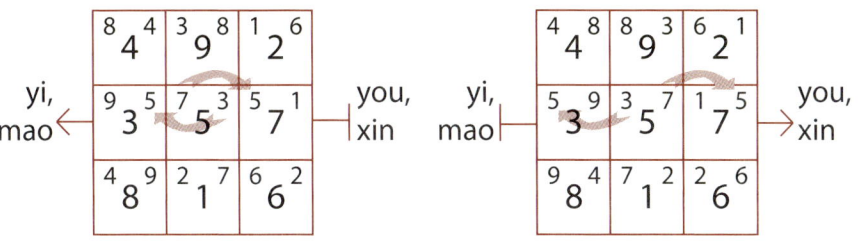

Fig-22: 3-7 at central palace

My teacher, Master Joey Yap, has a unique interpretation that adds an interesting twist to the tale. He postulates that the term "fighting a battle (交戰)" could have been "crossing the *ji* (交戟)" originally.

A *ji* is a weapon having a long wooden shaft fitted with a spear head and a crescent blade at the top end. This weapon was used by guards at the city gates, who would cross a pair of *ji* to deny entry to unwanted visitors.

So instead of leading armies to victory, the commander finds himself being turned away at all 4 quadrants of the map. Chances are the man is a mercenary with shifting loyalties. A very different scenario indeed.

In other words, 3-7 could produce infamous dogs-of-war (mercenaries) or double-agents if the Stars are untimely or hurt by negative landforms.

There used to be a *fengshui* custom that could be traced back to Line SX83. Traditionally, tombs of high ranking military officers were aligned to the *jia-geng* axis, in the belief that their future generations could also become great military commanders. By the same reckoning, civilians usually avoided having their tombs or houses aligned to *jia-geng*. By and large, Chinese culture favoured civil service over a military career for their sons.

Some old masters probably thought "Long *geng*" referred to *geng* Mountain on the *luo pan*. We now know that is incorrect, but astronomical knowledge was not so commonplace back then.

Chapter 16: Special P5 Charts

Chapter 16 – Summary

- 2 Period-5 charts with 9-1 at the centre are exceptionally good for people matters and wealth.

- 2 other Period-5 charts that have 7-3 at the centre are capable of producing great generals, or infamous mercenaries.

Chapter 17
Double Sitting, Double Facing

CHAPTER 17:
Double Sitting, Double Facing

> **SX84:** 健而動，順而動，動非佳兆。
>
> If the strong is moving and the compliant is also moving, then movement is not a good omen.
>
> [章作：健而動，動非佳兆。
>
> Zhang's version: If the strong is moving, movement is not a good omen.]

The text gets lyrical and the use of metaphors takes on a new and complex dimension…

In Line SX84, the words "strong (健)" and "compliant (順)" invoke a statement from the *yi jing* (易經) treatise "Speaking of Hexagrams (說卦傳)" that says "*qian* is to be strong, *kun* is to comply (乾健也，坤順也)". The word "strong" can therefore be replaced with "*qian*", and the word "compliant" with "*kun*".

Neither do the Trigrams *qian* and *kun*, in this context, refer to the geographical locations Northwest and Southwest. Instead *qian* stands for the heavens, male, the ultimate *yang*, etc.; and in contrast *kun* stands for the earth, female, the ultimate *yin*, etc.

Pursuing this line of thought, the word "strong" represents the prosperous Facing Star; and the word "compliant" represents the prosperous Sitting Star.

The word "moving" refers to the *yang* side of the property, which is normally the Facing palace. It also implies that the landscape out front is wide open, possibly with water, but no mountains.

With that insight, Line SX84 is interpreted to mean that if both the prosperous Facing Star and prosperous Sitting Star are located at the Facing palace, then it is not that good. This is the case with "Double Facing (雙星到向)" charts.

Chapter 17: Double Sitting, Double Facing

Note that the line doesn't condemn the chart. It simply means that the prosperous Facing Star is supported by the *yang* environment out front, but the prosperous Sitting Star is not. Such a chart is good for wealth but not good for people matters.

It takes a hill at the far end of the open space to remedy the situation, at least to some extent. A natural hill is preferred, but failing that a building should also do the trick. In landform *fengshui*, this is called a "Table Mountain". A "Table Mountain" is mandatory in all situations, as otherwise the *qi* cannot be contained in front of the property.

In Zhang's version of the line, the second phrase is missing. This renders the line incomprehensible. A transcription error perhaps. Zhang's annotation of this line is unusually wooly, to say the least.

Chapter 17: Double Sitting, Double Facing

> **SX85:** 止而靜，順而靜，靜亦不宜。
>
> If movement has stopped and is still, and the compliant is also still, then stillness too is undesirable.
>
> [章作：止而靜，靜亦不宜。
>
> Zhang's version: If movement has stopped and is still, then stillness too is undesirable.]

Continuing our excursion down lyrical Wonderland… [Will someone please tell me if Alice did eventually catch that damn rabbit? ☺]

In the *yi jing* treatise "Speaking of Hexagrams", the word "stopped (止)" is associated with the Trigram *gen* (艮止也). This only adds to the confusion, as *gen* is irrelevant in the present context. Shen Zu Mian (沈祖綿) suggested that the word could be a transcriptional error, and should have been "moving (健)" instead.

My view is that the author did not wish to duplicate the first word in 2 adjoining lines, and chose the word "stop" simply to mean the end of movement, i.e. still linked to the word "moving". Granted it is a matter of conjecture, but not that farfetched.

Just as the word "moving" refers to the Facing palace in the previous line, the word "still" in the present line refers to the Sitting palace. It also implies that the landscape at the rear is mountainous and relatively dense, i.e. quite *yin*.

Following on from Line SX84, Line SX85 says that to have both the prosperous Sitting Star and prosperous Facing Star at the Sitting palace is not desirable either. This of course refers to "Double Sitting (雙星到坐)" charts supported by a *yin* environment at the rear. The prosperous Sitting Star is supported but not the prosperous Facing Star, i.e. good for people matters, not good for wealth.

Such charts are redeemed if there is flat land, or water if Indirect Spirit, at the rear before the ground rises.

As with the previous line, the omission of the second phrase in Zhang's version doesn't help.

Chapter 17: Double Sitting, Double Facing

Chapter 17 – Summary

➢ "Double Facing" charts (prosperous Sitting and Facing Stars both at Facing palace) benefit wealth but not people matters.

➢ "Double Sitting" charts (prosperous Sitting and Facing Stars both at Sitting palace) benefit people matters but not wealth.

Chapter 18
Rich & Famous

CHAPTER 18:
Rich & Famous

SX86: 富並陶朱，斷是堅金遇土。

If one's wealth matches Tao Zhu's, the explanation lies in tough Metal meeting Earth.

[章作：富並陶朱，斷是堆金積玉。

Zhang's version: If one's wealth matches Tao Zhu's, it is a case of "piling up gold and accumulating jade" (idiom meaning stupendous wealth).]

In Chinese folklore, "Tao Zhu Gong (陶朱公)" is the patron saint of merchants, reputedly a fabulously rich businessman and philanthropist. (See sidebar)

"Tough Metal meeting Earth" is an expression meaning *geng* (庚) seeing *wu* (戊) or *ji* (己). In Flying Stars terms, that would be 6-8 or 6-2.

Earth grows metal. Although unsaid, the line implies that the Star conjunction occurs at the Facing palace, as it deals with wealth. The timeliness of Star-6 and adequate support by landforms are also assumed.

Between 6-8 and 6-2, 6-2 is superior, as it is far easier to extract metal from soft earth than hard rock. Moreover, 6-2 produces the Hexagram "Unity (泰)", which is one of the most auspicious of the 64 Hexagrams.

> In the "Spring-Autumn Period" of Chinese history (770~476BCE), there was a folk hero by the name of Fan Li (范蠡), who gave up a high position in court to become a businessman.
>
> Fan applied his political skills to business and became hugely successful. He pioneered the concepts of meeting market demand, quality assurance and cash flow management, all of which were unheard of in those days.
>
> Fan was also known for his philanthropic work.
>
> As he set up his business at the town of "Tao (陶)", and took the name "Zhu (朱)", people addressed him by the honorific "Tao Zhu Gong (陶朱公)".
>
> For his business acumen and generosity, he was commemorated as the patron saint of merchants.

Chapter 18: Rich & Famous

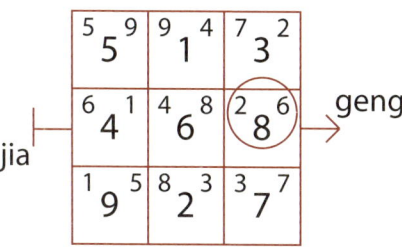

Fig-23: fabulous wealth

If all 3 Stars 6, 2 and 8 are present at the same palace, then the potential for wealth is phenomenal. See Fig-23: Period-6 property sitting *jia* facing *geng*.

Zhang's version is much less lucid. Taking the phrase "piling up gold and accumulating jade" at its idiomatic meaning is simply stating the obvious – not at all helpful. Even if we take the phrase at its face value and treat "gold" as Metal and "jade" (a hard stone) as Earth, it is more likely *xin* Metal (Star-7) and *wu* Earth (Star-8). So we have 7-8. The story doesn't gel.

Chapter 18: Rich & Famous

> **SX87:** 貴比王謝，總緣喬木扶桑。
>
> If one's status is comparable to Wang Xie's (idiom meaning high society), it is like a tall flowering tree.
>
> [章作：貴比王謝，總緣喬木扶疏。
>
> Zhang's version: If one's status is comparable to Wang Xie's, it is like a tall tree with luxuriant foliage.]

"Wang Xie (王謝)" is an idiom referring to the highest echelons of society. See sidebar.

"Tall tree" = Star-3; "flowering" or "luxuriant foliage" = Star-4, both timely.

[Strictly, "扶桑" is the Chinese name for the hibiscus flower, but a hibiscus tree is not that tall. So "tall flowering tree" makes a better translation in this instance.]

The conjunction 3-4, even if timely, would at best indicate a well matched couple. It's a long stretch to tie that to high society.

Several writers have this to say: in a Period-3 property sitting *mao* facing *you*, Facing Star-3 arrives at the Facing palace. Facing Star-4 resides at the adjacent *qian* palace. Now if water is seen outside *dui* stretching all the way to *qian*, then the 2 Facing Stars are linked. We have an effective, even if indirect, 3-4 conjunction (Fig-24).

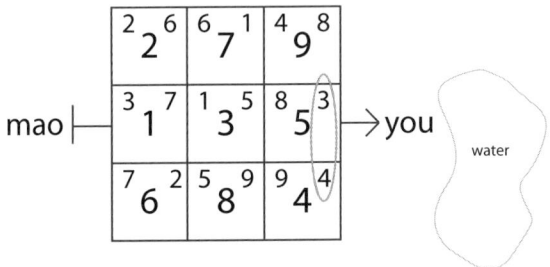

Fig-24: lofty status

The chart indicates that wealth accumulation will continue for 40 years, from Period-3 through Period-4. That should make the occupants pretty rich, and wealth can certainly buy some status, but enough to take them to the top echelons? The writers didn't explain, and I really don't think this makes a good example at all.

Chapter 18: Rich & Famous

Wang Xie (王謝) is not one person but 2 family names, Wang and Xie, linked together.

Wang Dao (王導) and Xie An (謝安) were tribal chiefs during the Western Jin (西晉) and Eastern Jin (東晉) Dynasties (4th Century CE). When the capital city at Chang An (長安) (present-day Xian) became indefensible, Wang persuaded the regent to relocate the capital to Jian Kang (建康) (present-day Nanjing). This led to the founding of the Eastern Jin Dynasty.

Wang became the Prime Minister and his family members also served in senior positions under several Jin emperors. He later recruited Xie An, who together with the latter's relatives, ably defended the country against further attacks and even recovered much lost ground.

The Wang and Xie families gained much recognition and power, and were firmly entrenched in the upper echelons of Jin society, even though they were originally tribesmen.

The saying goes that if one were able to compare oneself with the Wangs and the Xies, one's status must indeed be lofty.

Secrets of Xuan Kong

Chapter 18: Rich & Famous

Chapter 18 – Summary

- 6-2, 6-8 are wealth indicators. 6-2-8 together suggests fabulous wealth.
- 3-4 when timely points to high social status.

Chapter 19
Any Facing, Crossing the Line

CHAPTER 19:
Any Facing, Crossing the Line

SX88: 辛比庚，而辛要精神。

xin compared to *geng*, *xin* has more intense energy.

[章作：辛比庚，而辛更精神。

Zhang's version: marginally different wording, same meaning.]

SX89: 甲附乙，而甲亦靈秀。

jia attached to *yi*, *jia* has more grace and vivacity.

[章作：甲附乙，而甲益靈秀。

Zhang's version: *jia* attached to *yi*, *jia* benefits grace and vivacity.]

The 2 lines should be read together.

These are very taxing lines indeed. Writers have different opinions. The mainstream interpretation, and by mainstream I mean *xuan kong* heavyweights like Shen Zu Mian (沈祖綿) and Kong Zhao Su (孔昭蘇), goes something like this:

Outside *dui* palace, a landform at the *xin* sub-sector will outperform a similar landform at *geng*. Likewise, outside *zhen*, a landform at *jia* will outperform one at *yi*. Now the landform may be a body of water or a mountain, depending on whether the palace is Facing or Sitting.

I find that interpretation rather superficial and short on substantive arguments. When the 2 lines are read together, it looks as if the author, Wu Jing Luan (吳景鸞), was teasing his readers, much like a school teacher telling his class, "See, it's so simple…"

Clearly *geng* and *xin* each has its own strengths and weaknesses, and similarly for *jia* and *yi*. A sweeping statement that one is better than the other is highly irregular. It is more likely a figment of literary diversion.

Chapter 19: Any Facing, Crossing the Line

A property sitting *xin* must be facing *yi*, and one facing *jia* must be sitting *geng*, and vice versa. What the lines imply is that both *xin-yi* and *geng-jia* are just as usable. It all depends on the Period. In certain Periods, *xin-yi* will return a "Prosperous Sitting Prosperous Facing" chart, and *geng-jia* an "Up Mountain Down Water" chart; whereas in other Periods, the reverse will be the case. In other words, a facing has to be selected based on the timing.

Although *xin-yi* and *geng-jia* have been singled out for mention in these lines, they are just by way of examples. The same principle applies to all Sittings/Facings.

This is the interpretation offered by the modern writer Ke Jian Cheng (柯建成). I agree with him.

[A literary note: in Zhang's version of Line SX88, the word "益 <*yi*>" (meaning "benefit") is used in place of "亦 <*yi*>" (meaning "as well") in the popular version. The 2 words are phonetically identical. In terms of poetic structure, the popular version is more coherent.]

Chapter 19: Any Facing, Crossing the Line

> **SX90:** 癸爲玄龍，壬號紫氣，昌盛各得有因。
>
> gui is the mystical dragon, ren is purple *qi* (vitality). Each has its own reason for prosperity.
>
> [章作：癸爲玄龍，壬號紫氣，昌盛各得有攸司。
>
> Zhang's version: *gui* is the mystical dragon, *ren* is purple *qi* (vitality). Each controls its own prosperity.]

"mystical dragon" and "purple *qi*" are simply metaphors for beneficial *qi*, or Stars.

This line in fact reaffirms the earlier 2 lines that any Mountain (as in the 24-Mountains of the *luo pan*), whether *yin* or *yang*, may be selected as a Facing, depending on the Period.

One of the early writers, Bao Shi Xuan (鮑士選), explained it very succinctly. His comment is worthy of a verbatim translation:

> 癸壬各有宜用之時，非癸向爲吉，壬爲凶。亦非壬向爲吉，癸爲凶也。故曰昌盛各有攸司也。

gui and *ren* each has its own usable time. It is not that a *gui* facing is beneficial and *ren* harmful. Nor is a *ren* facing beneficial and *gui* harmful. Hence it is said each controls its own prosperity.

Chapter 19: Any Facing, Crossing the Line

> **SX91:** 丙臨文曲，丁近傷官，人財因之耗乏。
>
> As *bing* approaches Literary Arts, and *ding* comes near Hurting Officer, both people and wealth will be lessened because of it.

"*bing* (丙)" is the 1st Mountain of the Trigram *li* (離). "Literary Arts" in this case refers to *si* (巳), the 3rd Mountain of the Trigram *xun* (巽). *bing* and *si* are adjoining Mountains on the *luo pan*, but they belong to different Trigrams.

"*ding* (丁)" is the 3rd Mountain of the Trigram *li* (離). According to *ba zi* theory, the "Hurting Officer" of *ding* is *wei* (未). *wei* is the 1st Mountain of the Trigram *kun* (坤). On the *luo pan*, *ding* and *wei* are adjoining Mountains but belong to different Trigrams.

The line between 2 adjacent Trigrams, any 2 adjacent Trigrams, is called a "Death & Emptiness Line (空亡線)". It is highly detrimental for the Sitting/Facing axis of any property to fall smack on this line. Both people matters and wealth will suffer.

Now Line SX91 uses the words "approaches" and "comes near". It implies that even if the property's axis falls somewhere close to a "Death & Emptiness Line", it is bad enough. But how close is too close? Traditionally ±3° is considered close.

There is another aspect to this: if a landform, say a mountain or body of water, straddles over *bing* and *si*, or *ding* and *wei*, then the landform is said to have "crossed the line". That is supposed to be negative, but how realistic? This topic is covered in Line SX09.

There seems to be a literary flaw in the couplet made up of Lines SX90 & SX91. The 2 lines appear to deal with unrelated topics, which is highly irregular. Wu Jing Luan (吳景鸞), was clearly an accomplished scholar who took great pride in his composition skills. For him to write such a mismatched couplet would be like a mathematics teacher forgetting his multiplication tables! Quite unthinkable.

A logical deduction could be this: the author meant to say that any Sitting/Facing axis is usable depending on the Period, except that an axis close to the boundary between 2 Trigrams should be avoided. There would then be a link between the 2 lines, strenuous as it may be.

One other possibility is that parts of the original text were lost, and later writers chipped in with their own renditions, often of inferior quality. Historically, the adulteration of old *fengshui* texts was fairly widespread, and "Secrets of *xuan kong*" could well have suffered the same fate.

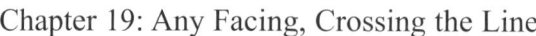

Chapter 19: Any Facing, Crossing the Line

Chapter 19 – Summary

- No one Sitting/Facing axis is intrinsically superior to another. In different Periods, different axes will return desirable ("Prosperous Sitting Prosperous Facing") charts.

- A Sitting/Facing axis very close to the boundary between 2 adjacent Trigrams is detrimental to people matters and wealth.

Chapter 20
Recalcitrant Stars

Chapter 20: Recalcitrant Stars

CHAPTER 20:
Recalcitrant Stars

SX92: 見祿存瘟癀必發。

Seeing "Rewards" will certainly cause an outbreak of jaundice.

SX93: 遇文曲蕩子無歸。

Meeting "Literary Arts" will cause the wayward son never to return.

SX94: 值廉貞而頓見火災。

"Chastity" on duty will quickly see a fire disaster.

SX95: 逢破軍而多虧身體。

Coming across "Broken Soldier" will seriously weaken the body.

"Rewards (祿存)" is the name of the 3rd star in the North Dipper Asterism (北斗星), and is an alias for Star-3.

"Literary Arts (文曲)" is the 4th star in the same Asterism, and stands in for Star-4.

"Chastity (廉貞)" is the 5th star, representing Star-5.

"Broken Soldier (破軍)" is the 7th star, representing Star-7.

These 4 lines take on a new pattern as they describe single Stars instead of Star conjunctions. There is a view that the lines should be read together with the preceding Line SX91. It is perceived that the *bing* and *ding* in Line SX91 refer to Star-9, and hence Line SX92 refers to 9-3; Line SX93 to 9-4; etc. I find this perceived association rather stretched.

Chapter 20: Recalcitrant Stars

In the practice of *xuan kong*, Stars are sometimes read singly. Their individual attributes are used to help explain or predict certain events. A whole paper can be written on this topic alone. It is by no means certain that Lines SX92 ~ SX95 are intended to provide a taste of that, but the departure from the norm is certainly intriguing.

The general perception of the 9 Stars is that Stars-1, 6, 8 are the good guys; Stars-2, 3, 5, 7 are bad; and Stars 4, 9 somewhere in between. By now, I hope readers are convinced that this general perception is wrong. Each of the 9 Stars can be beneficial or otherwise depending on the timing and the landform support it receives.

Yet Lines SX92 ~ SX95 describe only negative attributes. For the descriptions to make sense, it must be assumed that the Stars are out-of-timing; and that the external landforms are antagonistic.

Line SX92 attributes the outbreak of jaundice to Star-3. Modern medical knowledge tells us that jaundice is a symptom often caused by hepatitis, a liver ailment. As Star-3 (Wood) is associated with the liver, the connection is made. Fair enough I suppose, but I would have thought a broken leg is a more direct consequence.

Line SX93 blames Star-4 for a person's penchant for aimless wandering. That is because of Star-4 represents the Trigram *xun*, the wind.

Line SX94 links Star-5 to a fire disaster. Although Star-5 in its terrestrial form is of the element Earth, the "Chastity" Star in the heavens takes on the Fire element.

Line SX95 says Star-7 hurts the health. That is because "Broken Soldier" is a Metal Star with destructive attributes, exemplified by a knife.

Chapter 20: Recalcitrant Stars

Chapter 20 – Summary

- An untimely Star-3 indicates liver ailments.
- An untimely Star-4 tells of aimless travel.
- An untimely Star-5 spells fire risks.
- An untimely Star-7 portrays physical harm.
- The above 4 statements are unjustifiably sweeping and need to be taken with a pinch of salt.

Chapter 21
4-Graveyards, 4-Growths

Chapter 21: 4-Graveyards, 4-Growths

CHAPTER 21:
4-Graveyards, 4-Growths

SX96: 四墓非吉，陽土陰土之所裁。

It is said the "4 Graveyards" are not beneficial, but that is for the *yang* Earth and *yin* Earth to decide.

[章作：四墓非吉，陽土陰土貴剪裁。

Zhang's version: It is said the "4 Graveyards" are not beneficial, but that is up to the noble cutting (as in cutting the cloth to make clothes) of the *yang* Earth and *yin* Earth.]

"4 Graveyards (四墓)" refers to *chen* (辰), *xu* (戌), *chou* (丑), *wei* (未).

This line, as well as the next, contains a thinly veiled jibe at *san he fengshui*, the author's favourite punching bag.

According to *san he*'s "4 Major Water Mouths (四大水口)" theory, *chen* is the Grave of the "Water Frame"; *xu* is the Grave of the "Fire Frame"; *chou* is the Grave of the "Metal Frame"; and *wei* is the Grave of the "Wood Frame". These 4 locations are only suitable for water exits and not for water entry. This is probably the origin of the Graveyards' unsavory and undeserved reputation of being inauspicious.

[In his haste to belittle *san he fengshui*, the author in fact betrayed his ignorance, for *san he* does not consider the 4 Graveyards inauspicious. On the contrary, a Graveyard facing can be very beneficial under the right conditions.

Let me quote an example from the "Heavenly Jade Classic (天玉經)":

辰戌丑未叩金龍，動得永不窮 *chen*, *xu*, *chou* and *wei* knock on the golden dragon, if it moves one will forever not be poor.

To see how this is applied, just visit some of China's historical sites that still thrive after hundreds of years.]

Of the "4 Graveyards", *chen* (辰) and *xu* (戌) are normally labeled as "*yang* Earth", and *chou* (丑) and *wei* (未) as "*yin* Earth". However, this is of little relevance to *xuan kong*. In the *san yuan luo pan*, *chen*/*xu*/*chou*/*wei* are all of

Chapter 20: Recalcitrant Stars

yin polarity. Hence the phrase "*yang* Earth and *yin* Earth" should not be taken at face value. It is more likely an oblique reference to the flight of the Stars: forward is *yang*; reverse is *yin*.

The syntax of Line SX96 is somewhat clumsy, but the intended message is that the "4 Graveyards" are not necessarily inauspicious. Whether a Graveyard Sitting or Facing is favourable or otherwise depends on flight plan of the Stars, whether reverse or forward.

A reverse flight plan will deliver the prosperous Star to the appropriate palace thereby producing a "Prosperous Sitting" or "Prosperous Facing" chart, which is favourable. A forward flight plan will deliver the prosperous Star to the opposite palace thereby creating an unfavourable "Up Mountain" or "Down Water" chart. This is a fundamental precept of *xuan kong* Flying Stars. (see Line SX04)

Zhang's version merely uses more flowery language to say the same thing.

Chapter 21: 4-Graveyards, 4-Growths

> **SX97:** 四生非凶，卦內卦外由我取。
>
> It is said the "4 Growths" are not harmful, but it is up to me to select the inside or outside of the Trigram.

This line follows on from Line SX96.

"4 Growths (四生)" refers to *yin* (寅), *shen* (申), *si* (巳), *hai* (亥).

According to *san he's* "4 Major Water Mouths (四大水口)", incoming water from the "4-Growths" is highly desirable.

The phrase "inside or outside of the Trigram" has attracted different opinions.

The more straightforward interpretation is: "inside" implies leaning towards the adjacent "Heavenly Dragon (天元龍)" within the same Trigram, and that's good or at least harmless; "outside" implies leaning the other way which means crossing the line to the next Trigram, and that's bad (see Line SX09).

Shen Zu Mian (沈祖綿) and others interpret "inside the Trigram" to mean the "Earth Plate (地盤)", i.e. the *luo shu* distribution; and "outside the Trigram" to mean the "Heaven Plate (天盤)", i.e. the Period Stars distribution. Their arguments are not quite pristine, but the overall message is clear: the goodness or otherwise of a Sitting or Facing, or the location of incoming water, whether at "Growth" or "Graveyard", is determined by the time factor. No one location is good or bad in perpetuity. This is the key difference between the *san he* and the *xuan kong* approaches.

Chapter 21 – Summary

- *chen*, *xu*, *chou* and *wei* are not always harmful facings; neither are *shen*, *you*, *si* and *hai* always beneficial. It all depends on the Period.

- If the Period Star and the Sitting/Facing axis act together to cause a Star, whether Sitting or Facing, to fly in the reverse *luo shu* path, then the prosperous Star will always end up at the desired palace. Conversely, if the Star flies forward, the result will be undesirable. This is an inherent feature of the *xuan kong* Flying Stars technique.

Chapter 22
In Closing...

Chapter 22: In Closing...

CHAPTER 22:
In Closing...

SX98: 若知禍福緣由，妙在天心橐籥。

To know the causes of misfortune or good fortune, the intricacies are to be found in the bellows of the Heavenly Heart.

[章作：若知禍福緣因，妙在天心橐籥。

Zhang's version: To know the reasons for... (the rest unchanged).]

This is the closing line of the whole text - somewhat abrupt and uncharacteristic of Master Wu's style. One would have expected at least a well formed couplet to round off his masterpiece.

The word "bellows (橐籥)" describes a primitive device that blows air into a fire by squeezing a leather bag.

"Heavenly Heart" refers to the central palace of a chart and its contents: the prosperous Star of the current Period; and the respective Period Stars of the Sitting and facing palaces.

The phrase "intricacies... in the bellows of the Heavenly Heart" conjures up an image that the Stars 1 to 9 are stored within the central palace, and when the bellows are squeezed the Stars are propelled into the chart to fill out the other palaces. The resultant Star distribution will then be a coded message that tells of misfortune or good fortune, if one knows how to read it.

This graphic image aptly summarizes the purpose of the whole text.

Master Zhang Zhong Shan (章仲山) wrote an elegant end-piece to his annotation, which I thought is worth translating ad verbatim:

青囊萬卷，總不出體用二字。體有山水之分，用有得失之辨。體有移步之不同，用有隨時之更變。用必依形而顯休咎，體必用氣而見吉凶。統之，體無用不驗，用無體不靈。必須形氣兩兼，默參九星生剋之理，以推休咎，方得體用之精微。此《秘旨》言體言用，縷析條分，闡發精詳，無微不入，非深得青囊之奧，河洛之理者，焉能道其隻字耶！

Of the 10,000 scrolls of "Green Satchel" classics, there

Chapter 22: In Closing...

is none that does not mention the 2 words "body" and "application". (In modern terminology, that would be "hardware" and "software".)

While "body" takes the form of mountains and water, "application" is characterized by realization and loss. Just as a "body" looks different when a number of steps are taken, an "application" changes with time. An "application" needs physical forms to reveal good fortune and bad, and a "body" needs *qi* to do the same.

All in all, "body" without "application" is inaccurate, and "application" without "body" is uninspiring. In order to foretell good fortune and bad, the physical forms need to be evaluated together with the *qi*, and with the tacit inclusion of the 9 Stars growth-versus-control theory. Only in this way will the intricacies of "body" and "application" be realized.

This volume, "Secrets of *xuan kong*", explains "body" and "application" issues clearly, point by point, leaving out none of the intricacies. Even someone untrained in "Green Satchel" secrets, or ignorant of the laws of "*he* tu" "*luo shu*", will be able to grasp the wisdom of each and every word therein.

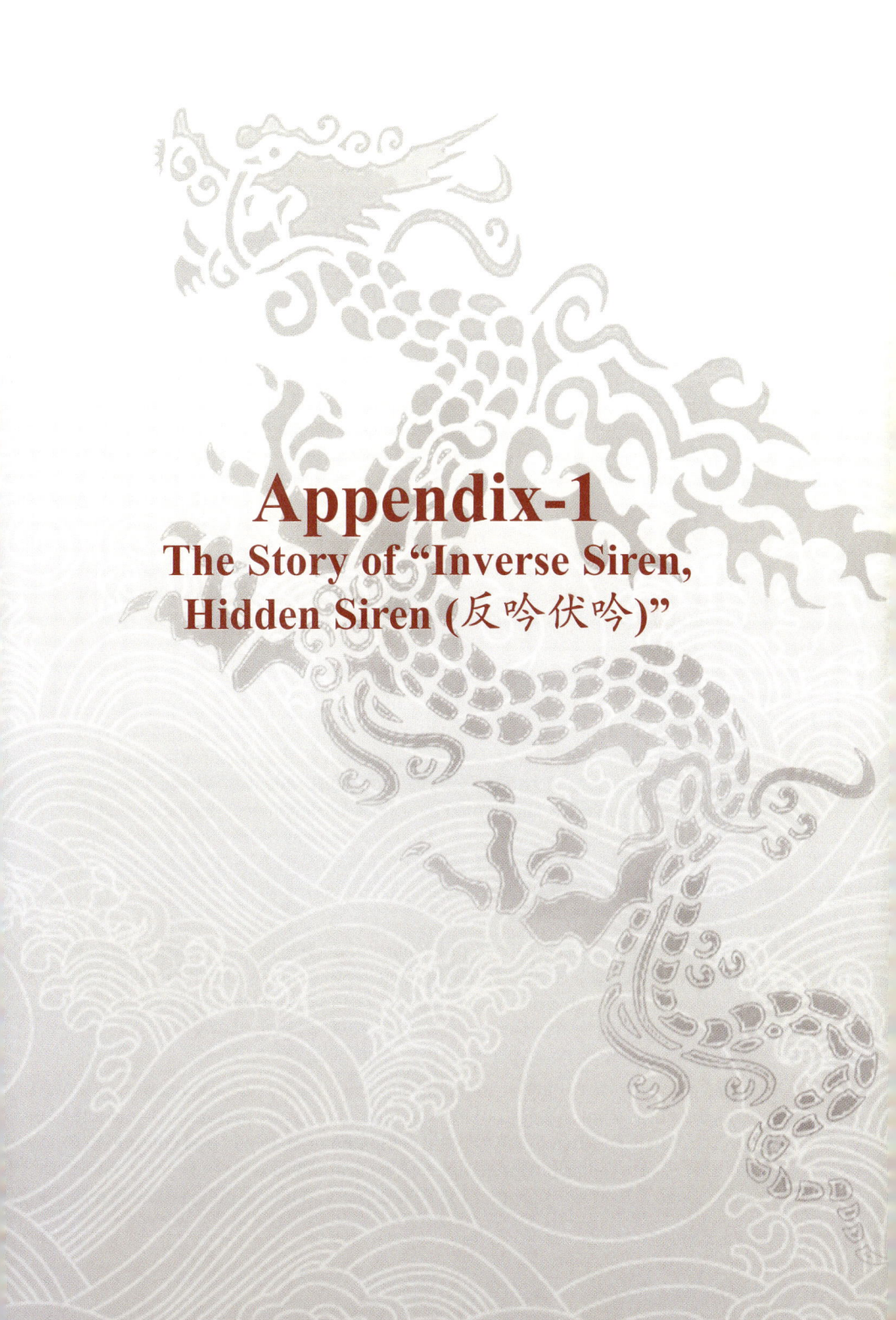

Appendix-1
The Story of "Inverse Siren, Hidden Siren (反吟伏吟)"

Appendix-1 The Story of "Inverse Siren, Hidden Siren (反吟伏吟)"

"Inverse/Hidden Siren" in *fengshui* is unique to *xuan kong*. The term probably has its roots in *ba zi* destiny analysis.

The following incident was recorded in the *xuan kong* classic "Shen's *xuan kong* Studies (沈氏玄空學)": In the winter of 1871, the founder of modern *xuan kong* Flying Stars, Shen Zhu Reng (沈竹礽, 1849~1906), located a plot of burial land that by *san he* principles had near perfect *fengshui*. Before he could buy it, the plot was snapped up by a local official with deep pockets, who then buried his parents in it. The tomb was seated *ren* and faced *bing*. Soon after the burial, the said official was disgraced and recalled for bungling a high profile case. He died en-route, and his family disintegrated. Shen was flabbergasted. How could such misfortune befall someone whose forebears were buried at such an auspicious site?

Later, he chanced upon a rare *xuan kong* treatise that mentioned a Period-1 property sitting *ren* facing *bing*, and vice versa, would violate "Inverse/Hidden Siren", and that could bring about rapid disaster. There was no further explanation. Shen was determined to dig deeper.

xuan kong at that time was a closed-door practice passed on from master to disciple under oath of secrecy. Shen read all the relevant material he could find, but got nowhere. In 1873, accompanied by his brother-in-law, Shen paid a visit to the famous *xuan kong* master Zhang Zhong Shan's (章仲山) family residence in Wuxi. By then Zhang had passed on, but a descendent of Zhang's was so taken by Shen's sincerity, augmented by a stack of banknotes, that he agreed to lend Shen a copy of Zhang's treatise "House Judgment (宅斷)" for a day. The 2 borrowers hand-copied the book overnight [clearly copyright laws weren't a big thing at the time, and they couldn't find a photocopier ☺].

At first Shen couldn't make much of Zhang's book, but in pursuing his *ji jing* (易經) studies, the idea of Star-5 leaving the central palace suddenly dawned on him, and with that awakening, everything in Zhang's book fell into place.

Shen made the study, practice and teaching of *xuan kong* Flying Stars his lifetime pursuit. Breaking with tradition, Shen taught the art openly. He conducted classes but did not publish anything during his lifetime. It was left to his son, Shen Zu Mian (沈祖綿), and contemporaries to edit and compile the elder Shen's papers, teaching material, and classroom Q&A sessions into a book called "Shen's *xuan kong* Studies (沈氏玄空學)". With the publication of this

Appendix-1   The Story of "Inverse Siren, Hidden Siren (反吟伏吟)"

book in 1925 and the rapid propagation of its teachings that ensued, Shen Zhu Reng became the publicly acknowledged founder of modern *xuan kong* Flying Stars.

[By the way, Shen Zhu Reng was quite proficient in English. He was brought up by a British army officer, and for a while made his living translating old Chinese military texts into English. He could have made life a lot earlier for us if only he had written in English!]

The mystery of "Inverse/Hidden Siren" was finally revealed in Shen's book, under a chapter entitled "Discussions on Inverse Siren and Hidden Siren (論反吟伏吟)".

By definition, a "Hidden Siren" occurs when the Sitting Star or Facing Star lands at a palace having the same *luo shu* Star, as for example Sitting or Facing Star-1 landing at *kan* palace (*luo shu* Star-1); or when Sitting or Facing Star-8 lands at *gen* palace (*luo shu* Star-8).

An "Inverse Siren" occurs when the Sitting or Facing Star lands at a palace that has the same *luo shu* Star residing at the palace diametrically opposite, as for example Sitting or Facing Star-1 landing at *li* palace, when *luo shu* Star-1 is at *kan* palace opposite.

When an "Inverse/Hidden Siren" occurs at a certain palace, that palace is said to have "violated Inverse/Hidden Siren (犯反伏吟)". If "Hidden Sirens" occur at all 9 palaces, the violation is said to be chart wide (全盤伏吟), which is clearly more onerous.

Strangely, if "Inverse Sirens" occur at all 9 palaces, it is not considered a violation at all. No explanation given.

Appendix-1 The Story of "Inverse Siren, Hidden Siren (反吟伏吟)"

The violations mentioned in Shen's book are tabulated below:

	Period	Sitting	Facing	Violation (HS="Hidden Siren", IS="Inverse Siren")
	1	壬	丙	Facing Star violates HS chart wide [This was the chart of the tomb that started it all.]
	1	丙	壬	Sitting Star violates HS chart wide
	9	壬	丙	Sitting Star violates HS chart wide
	9	丙	壬	Facing Star violates HS chart wide

Appendix-1   The Story of "Inverse Siren, Hidden Siren (反吟伏吟)"

	Period	Sitting	Facing	Violation (HS="Hidden Siren", IS="Inverse Siren")
	2	艮,寅	坤,申	Sitting Star violates HS chart wide
	2	坤,申	艮,寅	Facing Star violates HS chart wide
	8	艮,寅	坤,申	Facing Star violates HS chart wide
	8	坤,申	艮,寅	Sitting Star violates HS chart wide
Readers are encouraged to plot out the rest of the charts for practice	3	甲	庚	Facing Star violates HS chart wide
	3	庚	甲	Sitting Star violates HS chart wide
	7	甲	庚	Sitting Star violates HS chart wide
	7	庚	甲	Facing Star violates HS chart wide
	4	巽,巳	乾,亥	Facing Star violates HS chart wide
	4	乾,亥	巽,巳	Sitting Star violates HS chart wide
	6	巽,巳	乾,亥	Sitting Star violates HS chart wide
	6	乾,亥	巽,巳	Facing Star violates HS chart wide

Secrets of Xuan Kong

Appendix-1 The Story of "Inverse Siren, Hidden Siren (反吟伏吟)"

Period	Sitting	Facing	Violation (HS="Hidden Siren", IS="Inverse Siren")
5	艮, 寅	坤, 申	Sitting Star @ Sitting palace violates IS; Facing Star @ Facing palace violates IS
5	坤, 申	艮, 寅	Sitting Star @ Sitting palace violates IS; Facing Star @ Facing palace violates IS

According to Shen, violating "Inverse/Hidden Siren" is more harmful than an "Up Mountain Down Water (上山下水)" chart. Violators stand to suffer family breakups and death. Evidently Shen was profoundly influenced by the tomb incident that launched his *xuan kong* Odyssey.

There is a **second form** of "Inverse/Hidden Siren". Instead of comparing the Sitting or Facing Star with the *luo shu* Star, the Sitting or Facing Star is compared with the Period Star at the same palace. For example, a Period-7 property sitting *mao* facing *you* will have Facing Star-8 at *qian*. Now Period Star-8 also resides at *qian*. This is regarded as a "Hidden Siren" violation between the Facing Star and the Period Star. In the same chart, Sitting Star-6 also violates "Hidden Siren" with the Period Star-6 at *xun*.

In the same way, a Period-8 property sitting *mao* facing *you* violates "Hidden Siren" (9-9) at *qian*.

Appendix-1   The Story of "Inverse Siren, Hidden Siren (反吟伏吟)"

These 2 charts are illustrated in Fig-A1.1 below:

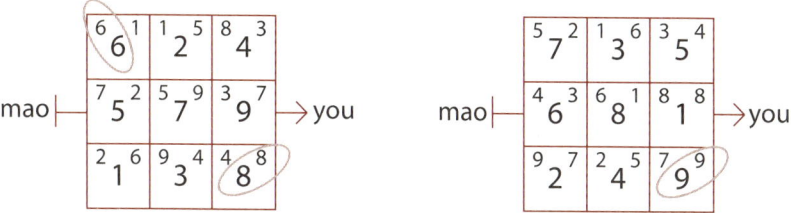

Fig-A1.1: "Hidden Siren" with Period Star

In the book "Shen's *xuan kong* Studies", this second form of "Inverse/Hidden Siren" violation was added by Shen Junior in what appeared to be an afterthought. Of course, Shen Junior was an accomplished *xuan kong* master in his own right, but the weight of coverage in Shen's and other texts suggested that this second form of violation played second fiddle to the original violation involving the *luo shu* Star.

According to Shen Junior, if the afflicted Star was timely, the "Siren" could in fact produce immense wealth (he was talking about the Facing Star), but when the Star's timeliness passed, the violation would surely inflict disaster, including sudden and violent death.

There is in fact a **third form** of "Inverse/Hidden Siren" violation that involves the 64 Hexagrams. It is sometimes called the "Gold Division (分金)" form of "Inverse/Hidden Siren". To explain the 64 Hexagrams would be quite outside our present scope. In the following discussion, I have to assume that the reader is familiar with the names of the 64 Hexagrams, and the ways in which the lines of a Hexagram may be transformed to form complementary Hexagrams called "Inverted Hexagram (綜卦)" and "Opposite Hexagram (錯卦)", as shown in Fig-A1.2 below:

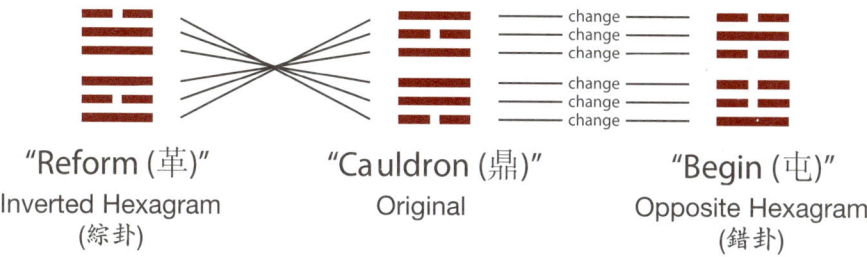

Fig-A1.2: complementary Hexagrams

Appendix-1   The Story of "Inverse Siren, Hidden Siren (反吟伏吟)"

One may well ask: what have Flying Stars got to do with Hexagrams? The answer lies in a procedure called "Swinging out a Hexagram (盪卦)", which is a way to extract a Hexagram from the Sitting and Facing Stars (in fact any 2 Stars) in a palace.

Let's start with assigning Trigrams to the Flying Stars 1 to 9, and giving them descriptive names, as follows:

Flying Star	Trigram	Description
1	☵	Water (水)
2	☷	Earth (地)
3	☳	Thunder (雷)
4	☴	Wind (風)
5	none	
6	☰	Heaven (天)
7	☱	Marsh (澤)
8	☶	Mountain (山)
9	☲	Fire (火)

For example, if a particular palace has Sitting Star-4 and Facing Star-9, we could "swing out" the following Hexagram from the combination 4-9:

The name of this Hexagram is "Cauldron (鼎)".

Fire over Wind

"Cauldron (鼎)"

Note that the Facing Star is always placed on top, and the Sitting Star below.

Appendix-1 The Story of "Inverse Siren, Hidden Siren (反吟伏吟)"

Star-5 has no Hexagram associated with it. If either the Facing Star or Sitting Star is a 5, it needs to be replaced according to certain rules:

- In any Period other than Period-5, Facing Star-5 or Sitting Star-5 at any palace shall be replaced by the Period Star at the central palace;
- In Period-5, Facing Star-5 or Sitting Star-5 at any palace shall be replaced by the Facing Star or Sitting Star, respectively, at the central palace.

Take a Period-7 property sitting *jia* facing *geng*. Fig-A1.3 shows the Flying Stars chart of the property, annotated with the 9 Hexagrams that have been "swung out" from the Sitting Star - Facing Star combinations.

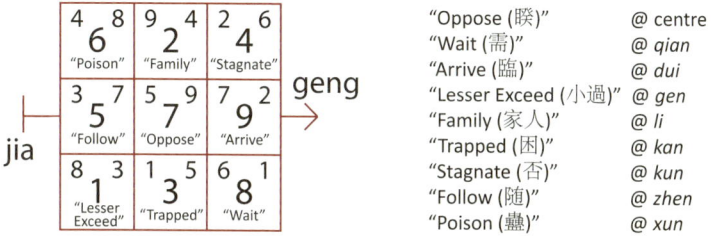

Fig-A1.3: Hexagrams in a chart

Note that the Sitting Star-5 at the central palace, and the Facing Star-5 at *kan* palace, have both been replaced by the Period Star-7, as shown below:

At the central palace, 5-9 becomes 7-9, hence

"Oppose (睽)"

At *kan* palace, 1-5 becomes 1-7, hence

"Trapped (困)"

Going back to Fig-A1.3, we see that the Hexagram at the Facing palace is "Arrive (臨 ☷)"; the Hexagram at the Sitting palace is "Follow (隨 ☳)"; and the Hexagram at the central palace is "Oppose (睽 ☳)".

Appendix-1 The Story of "Inverse Siren, Hidden Siren (反吟伏吟)"

The next step is to derive the complementary "Inverted Hexagram" and "Opposite Hexagram" of these 3 Hexagrams, as follows:

Original Hexagram	Inverted Hexagram (綜卦)	Opposite Hexagram (錯卦)
Arrive (臨 ䷒)	Observe (觀 ䷓)	Retreat (遯 ䷠)
Follow (隨 ䷐)	Poison (蠱 ䷑)	Poison (蠱 ䷑)
Oppose (睽 ䷥)	Family (家人 ䷤)	Obstruct (蹇 ䷦)

[Sometimes the "Inverted Hexagram" and "Opposite Hexagram" are the same, as in the case of "Follow" above.]

We need to check that the property's facing and sitting directions do not clash with any of the "Inverted Hexagrams" and "Opposite Hexagrams" derived above. To do this we have to measure the facing of the property using a *san yuan luo pan* or a specialist *xuan kong luo pan*.

Appendix-1 The Story of "Inverse Siren, Hidden Siren (反吟伏吟)"

For this purpose, the outer 64-Hexagram ring of the *luo pan* is used. This ring is illustrated in Fig-A1.4 (outermost ring).

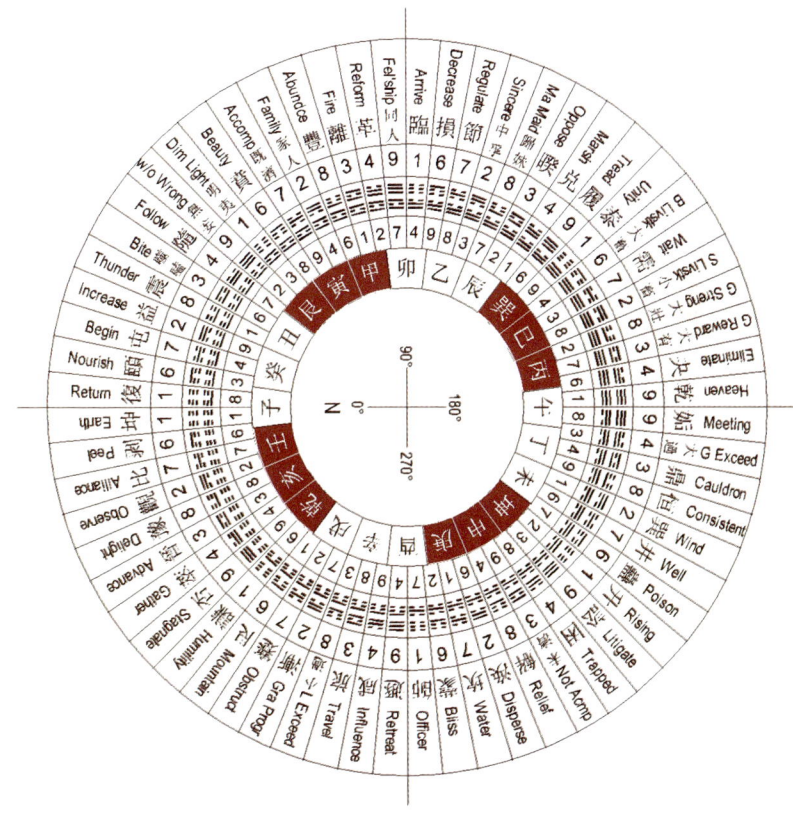

Fig-A1.4: 64-Hexagram ring

Stand at the property's fascia and measure the facing in the usual manner. Observe where the red string of the *luo pan* (the one perpendicular to the fascia) falls on this ring. The Hexagram under the red string in the facing direction is the Facing Hexagram, and the Hexagram at the opposite end of the same string is the Sitting Hexagram. Note that these 2 Hexagrams are always in opposition, i.e. one is the "Opposite Hexagram" of the other.

If the Facing Hexagram read from the *luo pan* turns out to be the same as the "Inverted Hexagram" of the Facing Hexagram in the chart ("Observe" in our example), the facing of the property is said to have violated "Hidden Siren".

If the Facing Hexagram read from the *luo pan* is the same as the "Opposite Hexagram" of the Facing Hexagram in the chart ("Retreat" in our example), the facing of the property is said to have violated "Inverse Siren".

Appendix-1 The Story of "Inverse Siren, Hidden Siren (反吟伏吟)"

If the Sitting Hexagram read from the *luo pan* is the same as the "Inverted Hexagram" of the Sitting Hexagram in the chart ("Poison"), the sitting of the property is said to have violated "Hidden Siren".

If the Sitting Hexagram read from the *luo pan* is the same as the "Opposite Hexagram" of the Sitting Hexagram in the chart (also "Poison"), the sitting of the property is said to have violated "Inverse Siren".

If the Facing or Sitting Hexagram read from the *luo pan* is the same as the "Inverted Hexagram" of the central Hexagram in the chart ("Family"), the property is said to have violated "Hidden Siren" as a whole.

If the Facing or Sitting Hexagram read from the *luo pan* is the same as the "Opposite Hexagram" of the central Hexagram in the chart ("Obstruct"), the property is said to have violated "Inverse Siren" as a whole.

To summarize, the Facing and Sitting Hexagrams read from the *luo pan* must not be identical to the "Inverted Hexagram" or "Opposite Hexagram" of the chart's Facing, Sitting and central Hexagrams.

It will be seen that there are no "Gold Division" violations in the case of Fig-A1.3. [But the Sitting Stars violate "Hidden Siren" chart wide with respect to the *luo shu* Stars, and Facing Star-7 at *zhen* violates "Inverse Siren". Moreover, it is "Up Mountain Down Water". Not a good chart at all.]

In fact there are not many charts susceptible to this form of "Inverse/Hidden Siren" violation, but it is prudent to check. An often cited example is a Period-4 property sitting *qian* facing *xun*, where the Hexagram at *qian* palace is "Unity (泰 ☷☰)". (Fig-A1.5)

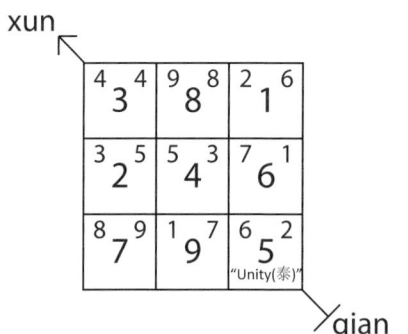

Fig-A1.5: Hexagram violation

The "Inverted Hexagram" of "Unity" is "Stagnation (否 ☰☷)". Hence if the Sitting Hexagram measured on the *luo pan* happens to be "Stagnation", i.e. compass bearing 315° ~ 320° approx, the property has violated "Hidden Siren".

[On reflection, this example is only good for learning purposes. In practice, the Sitting Star-6 at *qian* palace (*luo shu* Star-6) already tells us the property has violated "Hidden Siren". So why bother with the Hexagrams? ☹]

Appendix-1   The Story of "Inverse Siren, Hidden Siren (反吟伏吟)"

Another example can be found in a Period-6 property sitting *wu* facing *zi* (Fig-A1.6). The Hexagram at the Sitting palace is "Heaven (乾 ☰)". The "Heaven" Hexagram upon being inverted is still "Heaven (乾 ☰)".

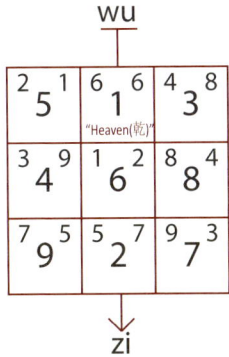

Fig-A1.6: Hexagram violation

If the property happens to sit on compass bearing 175°~180° approx, at which the Hexagram "Heaven" of the *luo pan* is located, then the property has violated "Hidden Siren".

This third form of "Inverse/Hidden Siren" is relatively easy to fix. Simply tilt the facing slightly to get out of the offending Hexagram. After all, a Hexagram only covers 5.625 arc degrees on the compass.

What is the cure for an "Inverse/Hidden Siren" violation?

Firstly, not all "Inverse/Hidden Sirens" need to be cured. Like any other Flying Stars taboo, a "Siren" is only harmful if it is collaborated by negative landforms or *sha qi* outside. Landforms to watch out for are deformed mountains, sheer cliffs, towering edifices, wind gaps, reverse bow (convex) water, rushing water, busy highways, T-junctions, etc. If the surrounding environment is serene and devoid of *sha qi*, the "Siren" will not be activated.

According to the classics, "Sirens" at the Facing palace are resolved by having water, or a roadway (virtual water) outside the Facing palace. If real water is used, it should be checked that the "Direct/Indirect Spirit" rule is not violated.

Appendix-1   The Story of "Inverse Siren, Hidden Siren (反吟伏吟)"

"Sirens" at the Sitting palace are harder to deal with. Several old texts hinted at possible cures, but none of them was very explicit about it. The hints implied that the problem could be resolved by the presence of certain beneficial Stars at the afflicted palace. These "white knight" Stars carry the jargon name "3 Stars 5 Beneficial (三星五吉)", and are time dependent, as follows:

- Upper Cycle (Periods-1,2,3): Stars 1, 2, 3, 6, 8

- Middle Cycle (Periods-4,5,6): Stars 4, 5, 6, 8, 1

- Lower Cycle (Periods-7,8,9): Stars 7, 8, 9, 1, 6

[This is not the only definition but the one that makes the most sense.]

Clearly these "white knights" are only helpful if they themselves are timely. For example, in Period-8, only 8, 9 and 1 can be used, not 7 or 6.

The "white knights" may come in various guises: Period Star, Facing Star, Sitting Star, Annual Star, whatever. A *xuan kong* master needs to be resourceful at problem solving. For example, a person of *gua*-9, a second daughter, or a young adult female can also be regarded as Star-9. If such a person resides at the afflicted palace, then the problem is resolved. [As beauty is also Star-9, I wonder if having a beautiful live-in girlfriend counts ☺]

"Sirens" at a palace other than the Facing or Sitting palace is less problematic. Having open space outside the afflicted palace is enough to resolve the problem. Moreover, such a "Siren" will only affect those persons who have an affinity with the afflicted Star. For example, a 2-2 "Hidden Siren" will only affect the mother, an old women or a *gua*-2 person. [Only Mother-in-law gets hurt, so never mind... Just kidding ☺]

A chart wide violation of "Hidden Siren" (at all 9 palaces) is potentially more destructive. If the property is, in addition, hemmed in on all sides by sheer cliffs or a concrete jungle, then disaster is bound to strike. In such a case, it is prudent to advise the occupants to move out.

"Shen's *xuan kong* Studies" and subsequent *xuan kong* texts only mentioned the 3 forms of "Inverse/Hidden Siren" described above, but *xuan kong* is a highly flexible art. In principle, there is no reason why any visiting Star to a palace cannot form a "Siren" with any other Star resident in that palace (except the Sitting and Facing Stars do not form "Sirens" with each other). The reading can become complicated though.

Appendix-1   The Story of "Inverse Siren, Hidden Siren (反吟伏吟)"

The modern interpretation is that a "Hidden Siren" represents a subtle warning, like a nagging doubt in one's mind that something is not quite right. Trouble will surface when a second "Siren", or another negative Star, or other form of *sha qi* hits the afflicted palace.

An "Inverse Siren" is more upfront. The antagonism is evident, and when trouble boils over, the outburst is often explosive in nature.

Note that the number pairs 1-9, 2-8, 3-7, 4-6 that make up "Inverse Sirens" are also "Later Heaven Combinations" ("Combo-10" numbers), which are supposed to be beneficial. So when is it a beneficial "Combo-10" and when is it a harmful "Inverse Siren"?

Judgment is required from case to case. If there is nothing to stop the combination from taking place, then the number pair should be read as a "Combo-10". However, if the intended combination fails for any reason, then the number pair becomes an "Inverse Siren". [Think of a spurned lover turning vengeful.] Situations that could break a "Combo-10" include the presence of 2 identical numbers fighting to combine with one potential partner; or a negative landform that would nullify whatever positive outcome from the combination.

from the ramblings of one hhc, a fengshui crazee
Revised Apr-2011

Appendix-2
"Castle Gate Formula (城門訣)"

Appendix-2
"Castle Gate Formula (城門訣)"

The "Castle Gate Formula" provides a quick acting technique for wealth. A property able to use this formula stands to prosper quickly even if the Facing Star at the Facing palace is unfavourable. The formula does not have the lasting power of a "Prosperous Sitting Prosperous Facing" chart though, but in these days when instant gratification is often demanded, the "Castle Gate Formula" could come in very useful.

There are 2 aspects to consider: landform (巒頭); and *qi* management (理氣).

First we have to establish whether a landform "Castle Gate" exists. By definition, a *qi* mouth located at either of the 2 palaces adjacent to the property's Facing palace is called a "Castle Gate". The confluence of 2 rivers is clearly a *qi* mouth; so is the point at which an Incoming Dragon releases a vein. In fact any landform feature, natural or man-made, at which *qi* gathers before being distributed will qualify as a *qi* mouth. In an urban setting, that could include:

– The confluence of 2 or more rivers, or monsoon drains. In classical texts, that is called "3-spoke water (三叉水)", and is the original and most potent of all *qi* mouths. The water must be exposed. Underground water doesn't count;

– A road junction through which traffic passes in order to enter or leave an area;

– A traffic island or roundabout, as it serves as a marshalling and distribution point for *qi*;

– An area surrounded by hills except for a gap at one location. This gap or opening becomes the *qi* mouth of that area. The same applies to a property seemingly encircled by other buildings;

– A villa or a gated community enclosed within boundary walls broken only at the gate. This gate is the *qi* mouth of the properties inside;

Appendix-2 "Castle Gate Formula (城門訣)"

- It is fairly common to have a slip road in front of a row of shop houses, and there is a road divider between the slip road and the main road beyond. Typically there are occasional openings in this road divider to allow traffic to enter or leave the slip road. If there is only one such opening visible from a given shop house, that opening could be treated as a *qi* mouth for that property. However if there are multiple openings within a short distance, then the *qi* is dispersed and we would not consider any of those openings a significant *qi* mouth;

- If there is a fair sized body of water or even a large fountain in, say, a residential development, the location of the water may be regarded as a substantial *qi* mouth, as *qi* gathers around water.

If any of the above *qi* mouths is located at either of the 2 palaces adjacent to the property's Facing palace, it is called a "Castle Gate"; but for this "Gate" to be used gainfully, we need to consider the *qi* management aspect as well.

In other words, there must be a landform "Castle Gate" in place first before we even consider applying the "Castle Gate Formula". Not all such "Gates" are usable. A *xuan kong* manoeuvre is applied to determine whether or not a "Gate" is useful. This manoeuvre is called the "Castle Gate Formula".

The "Castle Gate Formula" is essentially a set of rules to test the efficacy of a landform "Castle Gate" in relation to a given property. In other words, is the "Gate" useful to the subject property, and if so, how useful?

Appendix-2 "Castle Gate Formula (城門訣)"

Let us address these rules one by one:

Rule #1: For a given property, there are 2 possible locations for effective "Castle Gates". These are the 2 palaces adjacent to the property's Facing palace, one on each side. See Fig-A2.1.

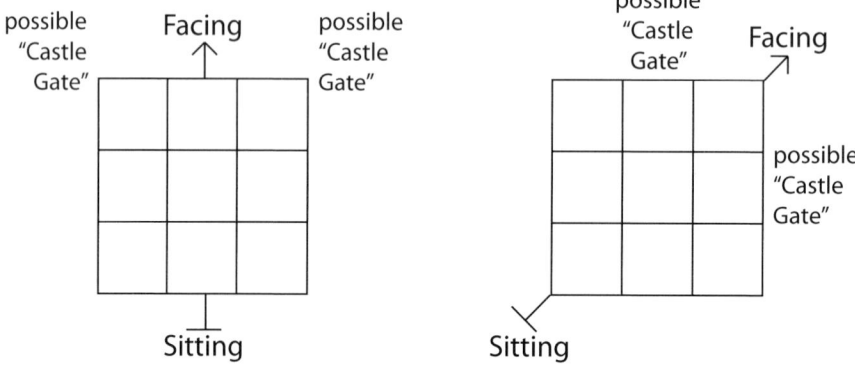

Fig-A2.1: Possible Castle Gates

Rule #2: For optimum effect, the location of the "Castle Gate" must match the property's Facing, in respect of the type of "Dragon", i.e. whether "Earthly Dragon", "Heavenly Dragon" or "Human Dragon".

Within each palace, there are 3 Mountains (*ren/zi/gui* in *kan* palace; *chou/gen/yin* in *gen* palace; *jia/mao/yi* in *zhen* palace; etc.). See Fig-A2.2.

ren, *chou*, *jia*, *chen*, *bing*, *wei*, *geng*, *xu* are classified as "Earthly Dragons";
zi, *gen*, *mao*, *xun*, *wu*, *kun*, *you*, *qian* as "Heavenly Dragons"; and
gui, *yin*, *yi*, *si*, *ding*, *shen*, *xin*, *hai* as "Human Dragons".

[*fengshui* texts are fond of using the word "Dragon" for a host of different entities, but really the word by itself has little meaning.]

Appendix-2 "Castle Gate Formula (城門訣)"

If the Facing of a property (and automatically the Sitting) is an "Earthly Dragon", then the "Castle Gate" should also be located on an "Earthly Dragon". Likewise, "Heavenly Dragon" "Castle Gate" for "Heavenly Dragon" Facing; and "Human Dragon" "Castle Gate" for "Human Dragon" Facing.

Combining Rules #1 & #2, a property facing *ren* can have a "Castle Gate" located at *xu* or *chou*; and likewise, a property facing *zi* can have a "Castle Gate" located at *qian* or *gen*; and so on…

Fig-A2.2: Earthly/Heavenly/Human Dragons

Rule #3: For any one Period, plot a chart with the current prosperous Star at the centre and the Stars flown in the forward order (often called a "Period Plate"). For example, a Period-8 chart will have Star-8 at the centre; Star-9 at *qian*; Star-1 at *dui*; and so on...

Take note of the Period Stars at the 2 palaces at which a "Castle Gate" can reside. Address each of these palaces separately.

We want to know if the prosperous Star (eg. Star-8 in Period-8) will arrive at the "Castle Gate" palace, after the Stars are flown in a certain way.

Appendix-2 "Castle Gate Formula (城門訣)"

From this point on, the method is best described by way of examples, as follows:

Example-1:

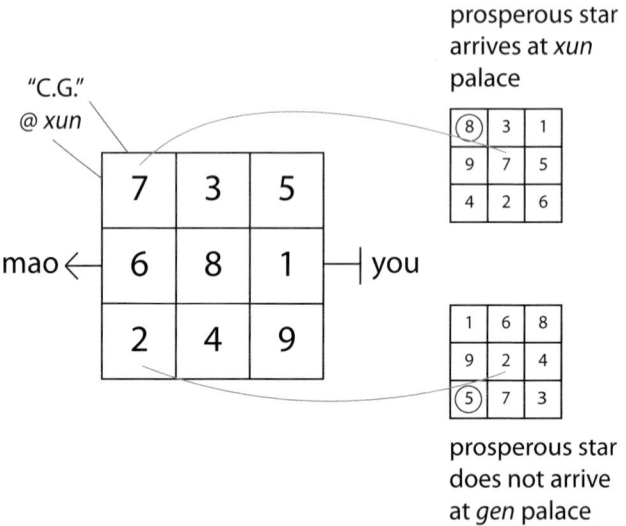

Fig-A2.3: Castle Gate @ *xun*, not at *gen*

Period-8 a property sitting *you* facing *mao* (Fig-A2.3) will have 2 possible "Castle Gate" locations at *gen* and *xun* (the 15° Mountains, not the palaces).

First check out *gen*:
Period Star at *gen* is Star-2, and it's a "Heavenly Dragon";
We know that for an even number, the "Heavenly Dragon" flies in forward order.

[Remember the mantra "plus/minus/minus for odd, minus/plus/plus for even" that we were made to memorize when we first learnt to plot a Flying Stars chart? It's the same thing expressed in a different way.];

Draw a separate 9-grid chart, and enter Star-2 into the centre;
Fly the Stars in forward order along the *luo shu* path;
It will be seen that Star-5 lands at *gen*;
Star-5 is not prosperous in Period-8;
Hence *gen* does not meet the requirements of the "Castle Gate Formula".

Appendix-2 "Castle Gate Formula (城門訣)"

Conclusion: even if there is a landform "Castle Gate" at *gen*, it will not benefit a *mao* facing property in Period-8.

Next check out *xun*:
Period Star at *xun* is Star-7, and it's a "Heavenly Dragon";
For an odd number, the "Heavenly Dragon" flies in reverse order.

Draw a separate 9-grid chart, and enter Star-7 into the centre;
Fly the Stars in reverse order;
Star-8 lands at *xun*, i.e. the prosperous Star arrives at the "Castle Gate" palace;
The "Castle Gate Formula" is satisfied.

Conclusion: a landform "Castle Gate" at *xun* will benefit a *mao* facing property in Period-8.

Appendix-2 "Castle Gate Formula (城門訣)"

Example-2:

In Period-8 a property sitting *wei* facing *chou* (Fig-A2.4) will have 2 possible "Castle Gate" locations at *ren* and *jia*.

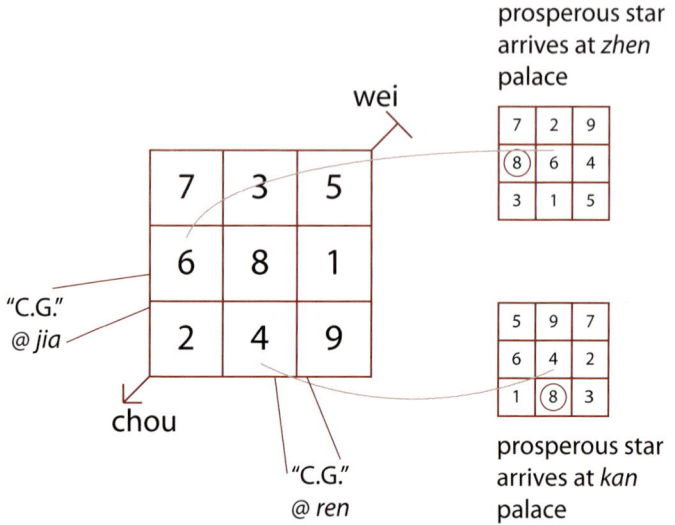

Fig-A2.4: Castle Gates @ *ren* and *jia*

First check out *ren*:
Period Star at *ren* is Star-4, "Earthly Dragon";
For an even number, the "Earthly Dragon" flies in reverse order;
Draw a separate 9-grid chart, and enter Star-4 into the centre;
Fly the Stars in reverse order along the *luo shu* path;
The prosperous Star-8 arrives at *ren*;
The "Castle Gate Formula" is satisfied.

Next check out *jia*:
Period Star at *jia* is Star-6, "Earthly Dragon";
For an even number, the "Earthly Dragon" flies in reverse order;
Draw a separate 9-grid chart, and enter Star-6 into the centre;
Fly the Stars in reverse order;
The prosperous Star-8 arrives at *jia*;
The "Castle Gate Formula is satisfied.

Conclusion: a "Castle Gate" at either *ren* or *jia* will be able to benefit a *chou* facing property in Period-8.

Appendix-2 "Castle Gate Formula (城門訣)"

It will be seen that every time a Period Star flies in reverse order, the prosperous Star will always arrive at the prospective "Castle Gate" palace; and likewise, every time a Period Star flies in forward order, the prosperous Star will not land at the required palace. So we can tell whether or not the formula is satisfied simply by looking at the Period Star at the "Castle Gate" palace (whether odd or even number), and the property's Facing (whether "Earthly", "Heavenly" or "Human Dragon"). We don't really have to plot out the chart unless it's for learning purposes.

Rule #4: The "Castle Gate" on one side of the property's Facing is more effective that its sibling on the other side.

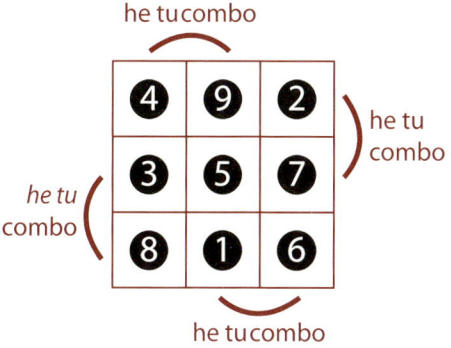

Fig-A2.5: Direct Castle Gates

Look at the *luo shu* chart in Fig-A2.5. The adjacent palaces whose respective *luo shu* Stars make up a *he tu* combination (1-6, 2-7, 3-8, 4-9) are marked. The "Castle Gate" that resides at the *he tu* partner of the Facing palace is called a "Direct Castle Gate (正城門)". The one on the other side of the Facing palace is called a "Secondary Castle Gate (副城門)". "Direct" is much more powerful than "Secondary".

[The old name for "Direct Castle Gate" was "Direct Horse (正馬)", and the "Secondary Castle Gate" was called "Borrowed Horse (借馬)". Rather fanciful names, but interesting.]

In *Example-2* above, the Facing palace has *luo shu* Star-8. The *he tu* partner of 8 is 3. Hence the "Castle Gate" at *jia* is "Direct", and the one at *ren* is "Secondary".

Appendix-2 "Castle Gate Formula (城門訣)"

In the case of *Example-1*, the Facing palace has *luo shu* Star-3. The "Castle Gate" at *xun* carries the *luo shu* number 4, which is not the *luo shu* partner of 3. Hence the "Castle Gate" at *xun* is only "Secondary".

Rule #5: Sometimes, a "Castle Gate" may in fact have a *he tu* combination hidden within.

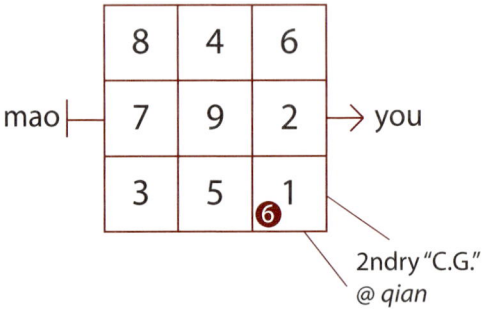

Fig-A2.6: Hidden *he tu*

Take the case of a Period-9 property sitting *mao* facing *you*. There is a "Secondary Castle Gate" at *qian* (Period Star-1). But the *luo shu* Star at *qian* is 6. So there is a hidden 1-6 combination in that palace (Fig-A2.6).

This hidden *he tu* combination enhances the efficacy of the "Secondary Castle Gate" and makes it almost as strong as a "Direct Castle Gate".

Rule #6: If Period Star-5 flies into a "Castle Gate" palace and sees water, then a *qi* mouth at that palace is deemed to be an effective "Castle Gate".

In Example-2 above, a *qi* mouth at *ren* is an effective "Castle Gate" in Period-8. Come Period-9, Star-9 enters the central palace and delivers Star-5 to *ren* (a component of *kan*). Will the benefits of the "Castle Gate" be lost? Not if there is an expanse of water outside *ren*.

When an incoming Star-5 sees water, it has a tendency to fly back to the centre, and in the process release the Star at the centre. In this example, the new Period Star-5 flies back to the centre and releases

Appendix-2 "Castle Gate Formula (城門訣)"

Star-9, which then goes to *ren*. Hence the *qi* mouth at *ren* continues to receive prosperous *qi*.

We don't need to fly Star-9 again, as it is already the prosperous Star of the Period. The "Gate" at *ren* continues to receive prosperous *qi*, and for all intent and purposes remains an effective "Castle Gate" in Period-9.

For this Star transposition to happen, the amount of water must be substantial. "3-spoke water" (river confluence) is best. A natural lake or series of ponds is fine. Man-made water must be at least swimming pool sized. The water should be already in place when the new Star-5 arrives.

[This same principle is invoked in 'curing' a "5-Yellow" (Annual Star-5) affliction at the Facing palace of a house.]

That more or less covers the essentials of the "Castle Gate Formula". The following are some topics for further deliberation:

Question: Rule #2 did say that the property's facing and the "Castle Gate" must be of like "Dragons". That is to say, for a property facing "Earthly Dragon", its "Castle Gate" must also be located at an "Earthly Dragon" Mountain, and likewise for "Heavenly Dragon" and "Human Dragon". How strict is that requirement?

Answer: A "Gate" that is contained within a single Mountain (15° on the compass) is said to be pure and strong, but in practice a landform "Castle Gate" often straddles multiple Mountains. In that event, there are several scenarios:

- A "Gate" that straddles between a "Heavenly Dragon" and a "Human Dragon" is tolerable as both "Dragons" are of the same polarity and both are within the same Trigram;

- A "Heavenly Dragon" crossing over into an "Earthly Dragon" suffers from mixed *qi* (same Trigram but different polarities), and is of much lower quality;

- A "Human Dragon" crossing over into an "Earthly Dragon" (different Trigrams) is unacceptable;

- An "Earthly Dragon" "Gate" must be contained within its own Mountain, because the adjacent Mountain on one side is of the opposite polarity, and the neighbour on the other side belongs to a different Trigram.

Appendix-2 "Castle Gate Formula (城門訣)"

[The old name for a pure "Castle Gate" is "Own Warehouse (自庫)"; and the name for a cross boundary "Castle Gate" is "Borrowed Warehouse (借庫)". I thought the correlation of a "Castle Gate" to a warehouse is insightful.]

Nowadays *xuan kong* masters are quite innovative. If a "Castle Gate" like, say, a road junction encroaches into an adjacent "Dragon", a wall or other structure may be erected so that only the desired "Dragon" is visible from the main door. Does this work, or are we just kidding ourselves? Well, each practitioner will have to take his own stand on the matter.

Question: Assuming we have a usable "Castle Gate", what do we have to do to ensure that the property benefits from it?

Answer: There must be a *qi* path, usually an approach road, to connect the "Castle Gate" to the property's principal *qi* mouth (main door). If there is no defined path, at least the "Castle Gate" must be visible from the main door.

Some practitioners take the view that in a modern high rise apartment, having a balcony or large window that looks out onto a "Castle Gate" will also work. After all a balcony or large window is also a *qi* mouth of sorts to an apartment.

Question: When will a "Castle Gate" kick in, and how long will it last?

Answer: The benefits of a "Castle Gate" will be felt almost immediately. If a property's Facing Star at the Facing palace is not timely in a particular Period, a "Castle Gate" will compensate for the deficiency very effectively. If the property already has a timely Facing Star at the Facing palace, a "Castle Gate" will further enhance its wealth prospects.

However, the benefits of a "Castle Gate" are relatively short-lived. It is only good for one Period. As soon as the current Period is over, its positive effects turn negative.

We can deduce that from the following consideration: during Period-8, a property sitting *wei* facing *chou* will have a "Direct Castle Gate" at *jia* (*Eample-2* above). When Period-9 arrives, the Period Star at *jia* will have changed to Star-7. Entering 7 into the centre of a 9-grid space and flying the Stars in forward order will deliver Star-5 to *jia*. Hence the *qi* coming from the "Castle Gate" at *jia* will have turned from prosperous to killing *qi* (unless saved by Rule #6).

Appendix-2 "Castle Gate Formula (城門訣)"

Traditionally, "Castle Gates" were used for immediate material gains. When the Period expired, the occupants moved out.

According to old *xuan kong* texts, one recommended use of a "Castle Gate" was for the burial of a deceased ancestor during times of civil unrest, when good burial ground was hard to find. Simply bury the deceased in a temporary grave that receives "Castle Gate" *qi*. The wellbeing of the family would then be protected immediately. Years later when peace has been restored, a permanent burial ground could be found and the remains reinterred.

In modern times, 20 years are considered plenty for an average residential house or apartment. Few people will think ahead far enough to worry about the expiry of a "Castle Gate".

For those who do, what can be done after the "Gate" has expired? The books have this to say: if the property's chart based on the new Period is "Prosperous Sitting Prosperous Facing", then undertake extensive renovations to change the Period of the chart. In this way the property remains good in the new Period. In practice such an option is rarely available.

From the ramblings of one hhc, a fengshui crazee
revised Mar-2011

Appendix-3
Star Conjunctions –
A Bird's Eye View

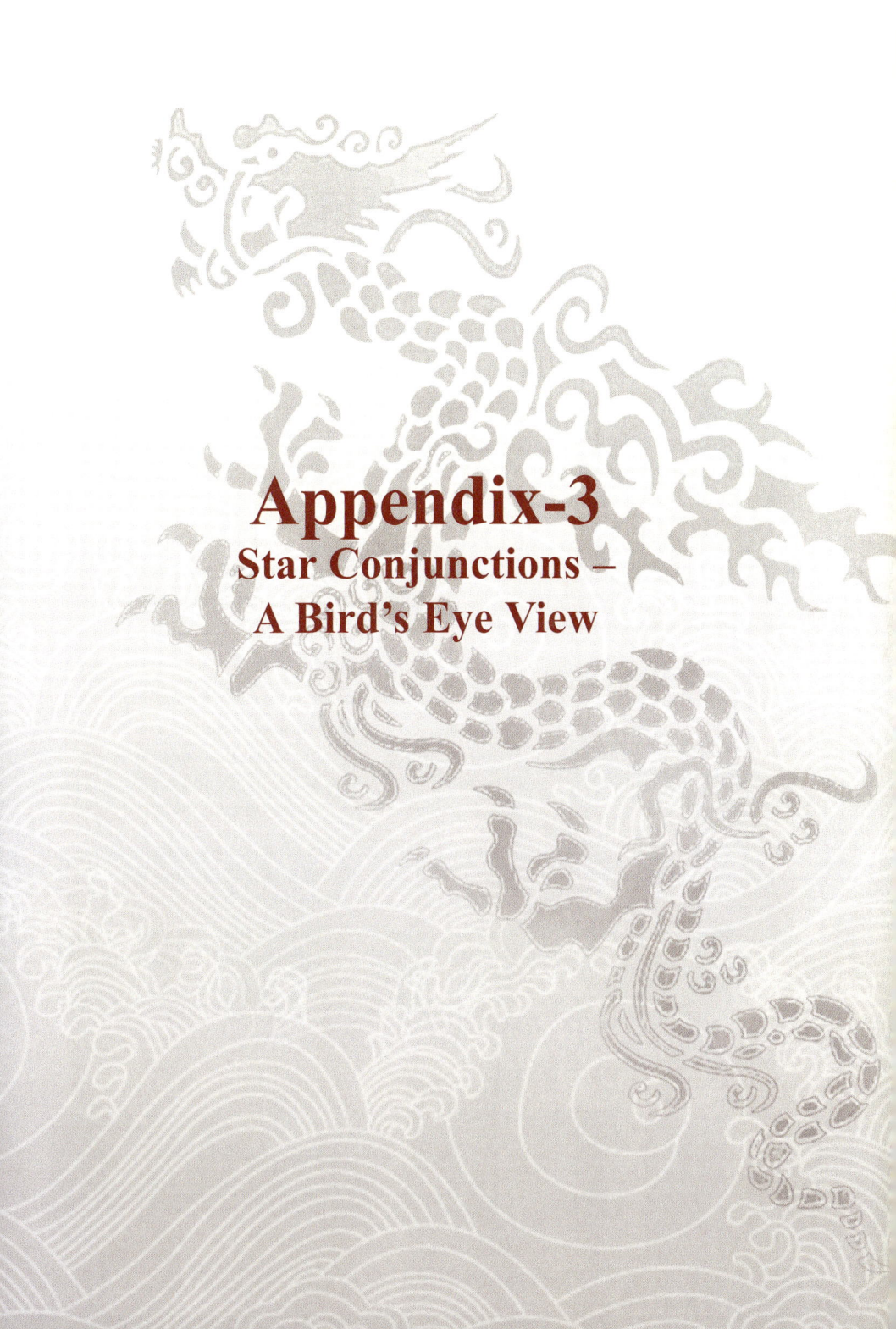

Appendix-3
Star Conjunctions – A Bird's Eye View

One of the most valuable features of "Secrets of *xuan kong*" is its repertoire of Star conjunctions. The conjunctions are however not presented in any particular order, and some are repeated sporadically all over the text.

I therefore decided to collate all conjunctions mentioned in the text and have them tabulated in numerical order in this Appendix, for easy reference.

For all intent and purposes, the text ignores the order of the Stars. That is to say, 1-6 and 6-1 are treated in the same way, as are 3-7 and 7-3.

Whenever a favourable prediction is made for any Star conjunction, it presupposes that the Stars are timely and supported by landforms. Likewise, when a negative prediction is made, it goes without saying that the Stars must be out-of-timing and/or unsupported.

It is also worthwhile to note that Star conjunctions are not limited to Sitting Star - Facing Star. In fact, any Star may be paired with any other Star at the same palace. In certain instances, even Stars in adjoining palaces are paired. Flexibility seems to be the name of the game in *xuan kong*.

	Stars timely, supported	*Stars untimely, unsupported*
1-2	➢ Earth-Water conflict avoided if Wood is strong [SX39]	➢ stomach, spleen or intestinal disorders if Metal Stars and real water present [SX52]
		➢ deafness, urogenital problems, constipation, unable to conceive, miscarriage, blocked arteries, Down syndrome, etc. [SX60]
1-2-6	➢ high office [SX32]	
1-2-7	➢ property wealth [SX18]	
1-3	➢ property wealth enhanced [SX79]	

Appendix-3 Star Conjunctions – A Bird's Eye View

	Stars timely, supported	**Stars untimely, unsupported**
1-5	➢ Earth-Water conflict avoided if Wood is strong [SX39]	➢ deafness, urogenital problems, constipation, unable to conceive, miscarriage, blocked arteries, Down syndrome, etc. [SX60]
1-6	➢ notable success in high office [SX13]	
1-6-8	➢ property wealth [SX18]	
1-7	➢ property wealth enhanced [SX79]	➢ drink & debauchery [SX15] ➢ exile or running away if water flows away [SX15] ➢ kidney & ear ailments, hemorrhage, incontinence, seminal emissions [SX15] ➢ flirtations & drink [SX72]
1-8	➢ Earth-Water conflict avoided if Wood is strong [SX39]	➢ deafness, urogenital problems, constipation, unable to conceive, miscarriage, blocked arteries, Down syndrome, etc. [SX60]
1-9	➢ a natural *luo shu* pair, favours progeny [SX25] ➢ the Stars' relationship with Early Heaven *qian* and *kun* encourages formation of Combo-10 [SX35] ➢ birth of an heir [SX77] ➢ 2 Period-5 charts with 9-1 at centre are exceptionally good for people and wealth [SX82]	➢ inability to conceive or miscarriage [SX22] ➢ blindness, cardiac problems, scalding, unstable temperaments, etc. [SX61]

Appendix-3   Star Conjunctions – A Bird's Eye View

		Stars timely, supported	*Stars untimely, unsupported*
2-3		➢ Wood-Earth conflict avoided if Metal is strong [SX37]	➢ "Bull Fight Killing" - quarrels [SX16] ➢ acts of terror & punishment [SX16]
2-4		➢ Wood-Earth conflict avoided if Metal is strong [SX37] ➢ humanity and human values thrive [SX78]	➢ daughter-in-law bullies the mother [SX56] ➢ abdominal disorders including stomach/spleen/pancreas, digestive problems, muscular pains, skin disease, gynecological issues, etc. [SX64] ➢ depression, hallucination, apparitions [SX64]
2-6		➢ a natural *luo shu* pair, favours progeny [SX25] ➢ great wealth [SX86]	
2-6-8		➢ stupendous wealth [SX86]	
2-8			➢ monks and nuns [SX80]
2-8-9		➢ wealth comparable with the national coffers [SX76]	
2-9			➢ stupidity [SX20]
3-4		➢ a natural *luo shu* pair, favours progeny [SX25] ➢ high social status [SX87]	➢ manipulation, deception, fraud, embezzlement [SX81] ➢ woman taking advantage of man [SX81]
3-6		➢ Metal-Wood conflict avoided if Fire is strong [SX39]	➢ fractured limbs [SX53] ➢ legs and fingers getting hurt [SX65]

Appendix-3 Star Conjunctions – A Bird's Eye View

	Stars timely, supported	*Stars untimely, unsupported*
3-7	➢ Combo-10 forms only when Star is timely and supported [SX36] ➢ Metal-Wood conflict avoided if Fire is strong [SX39] ➢ civil & military power; excelling in studies and sports [SX74] ➢ 2 Period-5 charts with 7-3 at centre produce great military commanders [SX83]	➢ rushing about with little achievement [SX21] ➢ liver or blood disorders [SX53] ➢ coughing blood if water enters from *dui* and exits at *zhen* [SX55] ➢ "Piercing Heart Killing" – robbery and punishment by the law [SX55] ➢ ailments affecting the liver, gall bladder, hair, body hair, nerves, etc. [SX65] ➢ betrayal & ingratitude [SX73] ➢ instead of great commanders, mercenaries and double-agents are produced instead [SX83]
3-8	➢ Wood-Earth conflict avoided if Metal is strong [SX37]	➢ damage to spinal column, fractured limbs, locomotive disorders, rheumatoid arthritis, neurological disorders, etc. [SX63] ➢ young children getting hurt [SX63]
3-9	➢ exceptional intelligence [SX19] ➢ rapid fame and wealth [SX31] ➢ property wealth enhanced [SX79]	

Appendix-3 Star Conjunctions – A Bird's Eye View

	Stars timely, supported	*Stars untimely, unsupported*
4-6	➤ Metal-Wood conflict avoided if Fire is strong [SX39]	➤ suicide by hanging if waterway or road from *xun* loops round to *qian*, or vice versa [SX54]
		➤ problems with the buttocks and left side of body [SX65]
4-7	➤ Metal-Wood conflict avoided if Fire is strong [SX39]	➤ ailments affecting the liver, breasts, nerves, respiratory system, alimentary canal, intestines, etc. [SX65]
4-8	➤ thinkers and philosophers [SX11] ➤ Wood-Earth conflict avoided if Metal is strong [SX37]	➤ aimless wanderers [SX11] ➤ rheumatoid arthritis, neurological disorders, etc. [SX64] ➤ young children getting hurt [SX64] ➤ mental disorders [SX64]
4-9	➤ exceptional intelligence [SX19]	
6-8	➤ humanity and human values thrive [SX78] ➤ great wealth [SX86]	
6-9	➤ Fire-Metal conflict avoided if Water is strong [SX38] ➤ high status & long life [SX75]	➤ child scolds its father [SX57] ➤ "Fire Burning Heaven's Gate" if at *qian* - harms elderly male [SX57]
7-8	➤ fabulous wealth [SX14] ➤ a natural *luo shu* pair, favours progeny [SX25]	

Appendix-3 Star Conjunctions – A Bird's Eye View

	Stars timely, supported	*Stars untimely, unsupported*
7-9	➢ Fire-Metal conflict avoided if Water is strong [SX38]	➢ drinkers & pleasure seekers, redeemable with Star-1 [SX12] ➢ enhanced fire risk, especially if Wood Star is present [SX17] ➢ cleft lip, toothache, cough, throat infections, speech impediments, lung infections, menstrual issues, STD, knife wound, etc. [SX62]
8-9		➢ stupidity [SX20]

from the ramblings of one hhc, a fengshui crazee
Dec-2010

Bibliography

Bibliography

Shen Zu Mian (沈祖綿)　　沈氏玄空學 (1925)

Shen Zu Mian (沈祖綿)　　玄空古義四種通釋 (1940)

Kong Zhao Su (孔昭蘇)　　孔氏玄空寶鑑 (circa 1945)

Ke Jian Cheng (柯建成)　　玄空指妙 (1997)

Zhong Yi Ming (鐘義明)　　玄空地理叢譚第五輯 (1998)

Zhang Jue Ming (張覺明):　玄空秘旨精解 (2000)

The book by Zhang is especially useful as it compiled the annotations of different writers past and present. This greatly simplified research and cross referencing.

About the Author

Hung Hin Cheong (孔憲章) was born in 1946 at Kuala Lumpur, Malaysia. He received his early education in Malaysia before continuing with his tertiary education in the United Kingdom. He graduated with a Bachelor of Science degree with honours (1st class) in electrical and electronic engineering from the University of Leeds, England, in 1969.

He built his career in the electrical industry, and held the position of Chief Executive at a large international electrical equipment manufacturer, before his retirement in 2001.

fengshui has been the author's passion for many years. He studied under several masters over the years, and was appointed an instructor with the Mastery Academy of Chinese Metaphysics founded by Master Joey Yap, teaching *fengshui* and date selection since 2006.

The author was privileged to be schooled in both English and Chinese from a young age. This provided him access to the wide spectrum of *fengshui* material available in Chinese, which he perused avidly, ranging from ancient classics to popular magazines. This, together with his upbringing in a family steeped in Chinese traditions, afforded him a rare insight into the cultural background of classical *fengshui*. This advantage and his bilingual competence put him in good stead to help propagate classical *fengshui* knowledge to the wider world.

The author's engineering training also enabled him to put abstract and often ambiguous metaphysical concepts into a structured, logical and practical framework. He has published a number of papers in the electronic medium, which demonstrated his skill in translating and explaining classical texts clearly and succinctly in his own inimitable style. They also showed he was not shy of speaking his own mind when certain old ideas were clearly inconsistent with modern realities.

His first book, the "*xuan kong* Purple White Script (玄空紫白訣)" published in 2009, was well received by the English speaking *fengshui* community. In this second book, he chose to tackle another celebrated *xuan kong* classic, the "Secrets of *xuan kong* (玄空秘旨)". This ancient classic predated the "Purple White Script", and used language that is archaic and unusually complex. The amount of research that went into translating the text and unravelling the mysteries therein has elevated the author's classical scholarship to a new height.

Further Your Xuan Kong Knowledge
Recommended Courses

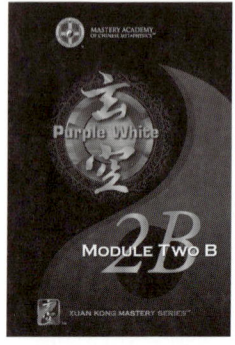

Xuan Kong Mastery Module 2B:
Xuan Kong Purple White Feng Shui

Purple White is a fundamental course that is essential to your understanding of Xuan Kong Purple White. Be guided by Joey Yap on the treasured secrets of the Purple White Script. Discover a powerful and vibrant form of Xuan Kong. It will transform the way you approach and practice Xuan Kong Feng Shui.

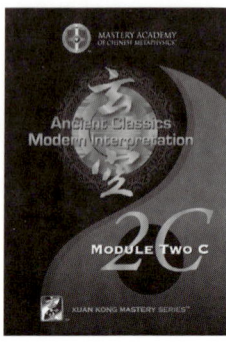

Xuan Kong Mastery Module 2C:
Ancient Classics Modern Interpretation

Focusing on decoding the secrets of the **Xuan Ji Fu** 玄機賦 or **Ode to Mysticism**, one of the four classic texts of Xuan Kong, particularly famous for its secrets to the Xuan Kong Life Palace divination technique. It also carries the hidden code to unlock a deeper side of Eight Mansions Feng Shui, and the secret to understanding the many Xuan Kong Hexagram combinations that allow the practitioner to, in many cases - predict outcomes and foresee the future. The secrets in this classic will allow you to penetrate a much, much deeper level of mastery in Xuan Kong Feng Shui.

www.masteryacademy.com /purplewhite

JOEY YAP'S
QI MEN DUN JIA
Reference Series

 **JOEY YAP**
Qi Men Dun Jia
Compendium
Second edition

 **JOEY YAP**
Qi Men Dun Jia
540 Yang
Structure

 **JOEY YAP**
Qi Men Dun Jia
540 Yin
Structure

 JOEY YAP
Qi Men Dun Jia
Year Charts

JOEY YAP
Qi Men Dun Jia
Month Charts

 **JOEY YAP**
Qi Men Dun Jia
Day Charts

 **JOEY YAP**
Qi Men Dun Jia
Day Charts
(San Yuan Method)

 **JOEY YAP**
Qi Men Dun Jia
Forecasting
Method
(Book 1)

 **JOEY YAP**
Qi Men Dun Jia
Forecasting
Method
(Book 2)

JOEY YAP
Qi Men Dun Jia
Evidential
Occurrences

JOEY YAP
Qi Men Dun Jia
Destiny
Analysis

JOEY YAP
Qi Men Dun Jia
Feng Shui

 **JOEY YAP**
Qi Men Dun Jia
Date, Time &
Activity Selection

 **JOEY YAP**
Qi Men Dun Jia
Annual Destiny
Analysis

 **JOEY YAP**
Qi Men Dun Jia
Strategic
Executions

 **JOEY YAP**
Qi Men Dun Jia
The 100
Formations

JOEY YAP
Qi Men Dun Jia
Sun Tzu
Warcraft

JOEY YAP
Qi Men Dun Jia
28 Constellations

 **JOEY YAP**
Qi Men Dun Jia
The Deities

 **JOEY YAP**
Qi Men Dun Jia
The Stars

  **JOEY YAP**
Qi Men Dun Jia
The Doors

 **JOEY YAP**
Qi Men Dun Jia
The Stems

This is the most comprehensive reference series to Qi Men Dun Jia in the Chinese Metaphysics world. Exhaustively written for the purpose of facilitating studies and further research, this collection of reference texts and educational books aims to bridge the gap for students who want to learn, and the teachers who want to teach Qi Men.

These essential references provide practical guidance for all branches under the Qi Men Dun Jia studies including Destiny Analysis, Feng Shui, Strategic Executions and Forecasting method.

These books are available exclusively at:
store.joeyyap.com

Email: order@masteryacademy.com | +6(03) - 2284 8080

JOEY YAP CONSULTING GROUP

Pioneering Metaphysics-Centric Personal and Corporate Consultations

Founded in 2002, the Joey Yap Consulting Group is the pioneer in the provision of metaphysics-driven coaching and consultation services for professionals and individuals alike. Under the leadership of the renowned international Chinese Metaphysics consultant, author and trainer, Dato' Joey Yap, it has become a world-class specialised metaphysics consulting firm with a strong presence in four continents, meeting the metaphysics-centric needs of its A-list clientele, ranging from celebrities to multinational corporations.

The Group's core consultation practice areas include Feng Shui, BaZi and Qi Men Dun Jia, which are complemented by ancillary services such as Date Selection, Face Reading and Yi Jing. Its team of highly trained professional consultants, led by its Chief Consultant, Dato' Joey Yap, is well-equipped with unparalleled knowledge and experience to help clients achieve their ultimate potentials in various fields and specialisations. Given its credentials, the Group is certainly the firm of choice across the globe for metaphysics-related consultations.

The Peerless Industry Expert

Benchmarked against the standards of top international consulting firms, our consultants work closely with our clients to achieve the best possible outcomes. The possibilities are infinite as our expertise extends from consultations related to the forces of nature under the subject of Feng Shui, to those related to Destiny Analysis and effective strategising under BaZi and Qi Men Dun Jia respectively.

To date, we have consulted a great diversity of clients, ranging from corporate clients – from various industries such as real estate, finance and telecommunication, amongst others – to the hundreds of thousands of individuals in their key life aspects. Adopting up-to-date and pragmatic approaches, we provide comprehensive services while upholding the importance of clients' priorities and effective outcomes. Recognised as the epitome of Chinese Metaphysics, we possess significant testimonies from worldwide clients as a trusted Brand.

www.joeyyap.com | +6(03) - 2284 8080

Feng Shui Consultation

Residential Properties
- Initial Land/Property Assessment
- Residential Feng Shui Consultation
- Residential Land Selection
- End-to-End Residential Consultation

Commercial Properties
- Initial Land/Property Assessment
- Commercial Feng Shui Consultation
- Commercial Land Selection
- End-to-End Commercial Consultation

Property Developers
- End-to-End Consultation
- Post-Consultation Advisory Services
- Panel Feng Shui Consultant

Property Investors
- Your Personal Feng Shui Consultant
- Tailor-Made Packages

Memorial Parks & Burial Sites
- Yin House Feng Shui

BaZi Consultation

Personal Destiny Analysis
- Individual BaZi Analysis
- BaZi Analysis for Families

Strategic Analysis for Corporate Organizations
- BaZi Consultations for Corporations
- BaZi Analysis for Human Resource Management

Entrepreneurs and Business Owners
- BaZi Analysis for Entrepreneurs

Career Pursuits
- BaZi Career Analysis

Relationships
- Marriage and Compatibility Analysis
- Partnership Analysis

General Public
- Annual BaZi Forecast
- Your Personal BaZi Coach

Date Selection Consultation

- Marriage Date Selection
- Caesarean Birth Date Selection
- House-Moving Date Selection
- Renovation and Groundbreaking Dates
- Signing of Contracts
- Official Openings
- Product Launches

Qi Men Dun Jia Consultation

Strategic Execution
- Business and Investment Prospects

Forecasting
- Wealth and Life Pursuits
- People and Environmental Matters

Feng Shui
- Residential Properties
- Commercial Properties

Speaking Engagement

Many reputable organisations and institutions have worked closely with Joey Yap Consulting Group to build a synergistic business relationship by engaging our team of consultants, which are led by Joey Yap, as speakers at their corporate events.

We tailor our seminars and talks to suit the anticipated or pertinent group of audience. Be it department subsidiary, your clients or even the entire corporation, we aim to fit your requirements in delivering the intended message(s) across.

www.joeyyap.com | +6(03) - 2284 8080

CHINESE METAPHYSICS REFERENCE SERIES

The Chinese Metaphysics Reference Series is a collection of reference texts, source material, and educational textbooks to be used as supplementary guides by scholars, students, researchers, teachers and practitioners of Chinese Metaphysics.

These comprehensive and structured books provide fast, easy reference to aid in the study and practice of various Chinese Metaphysics subjects including Feng Shui, BaZi, Yi Jing, Zi Wei, Liu Ren, Ze Ri, Ta Yi, Qi Men Dun Jia and Mian Xiang.

The Chinese Metaphysics Compendium

At over 1,000 pages, the Chinese Metaphysics Compendium is a unique one-volume reference book that compiles ALL the formulas relating to Feng Shui, BaZi (Four Pillars of Destiny), Zi Wei (Purple Star Astrology), Yi Jing (I-Ching), Qi Men (Mystical Doorways), Ze Ri (Date Selection), Mian Xiang (Face Reading) and other sources of Chinese Metaphysics.

It is presented in the form of easy-to-read tables, diagrams and reference charts, all of which are compiled into one handy book. This first-of-its-kind compendium is presented in both English and its original Chinese language, so that none of the meanings and contexts of the technical terminologies are lost.

The only essential and comprehensive reference on Chinese Metaphysics, and an absolute must-have for all students, scholars, and practitioners of Chinese Metaphysics.

The Ten Thousand Year Calendar (Pocket Edition)	The Ten Thousand Year Calendar	Dong Gong Date Selection	The Date Selection Compendium	Plum Blossoms Divination Reference Book	Xuan Kong Da Gua Ten Thousand Year Calendar	San Yuan Dragon Gate Eight Formations Water Method

BaZi Hour Pillar Useful Gods - Wood	BaZi Hour Pillar Useful Gods - Fire	BaZi Hour Pillar Useful Gods - Earth	BaZi Hour Pillar Useful Gods - Metal	BaZi Hour Pillar Useful Gods - Water	Xuan Kong Da Gua Structures Reference Book	Xuan Kong Da Gua 64 Gua Transformation Analysis

BaZi Structures and Structural Useful Gods - Wood	BaZi Structures and Structural Useful Gods - Fire	BaZi Structures and Structural Useful Gods - Earth	BaZi Structures and Structural Useful Gods - Metal	BaZi Structures and Structural Useful Gods - Water	Earth Study Discern Truth Second Edition	Eight Mansions Bright Mirror

Secret of Xuan Kong	Ode to Flying Stars	Xuan Kong Purple White Script	Ode to Mysticism	The Yin House Handbook	Water Water Everywhere	Xuan Kong Da Gua Not Exactly For Dummies

www.masteryacademy.com | +6(03) - 2284 8080

SAN YUAN QI MEN XUAN KONG DA GUA
Reference Series

San Yuan Qi Men Xuan Kong Da Gua **Compendium**

San Yuan Qi Men Xuan Kong Da Gua **540 Yang Structure**

San Yuan Qi Men Xuan Kong Da Gua **540 Yin Structure**

Xuan Kong Flying Star **Secrets Of The 81 Combinations**

Xuan Kong Da Gua **Fixed Yao Method**

Xuan Kong Da Gua **Flying Yao Method**

Xuan Kong Da Gua **6 Relationships Method**

Xuan Kong Flying Star **Purple White Script's Advanced Star Charts**

The **San Yuan Qi Men Xuan Kong Da Gua Series** is written for the advanced learners in mind. Unlock the secrets to this highly exclusive art and seamlessly integrate both Qi Men Dun Jia and the Xuan Kong Da Gua 64 Hexagrams into one unified practice for effective applications.

This collection is an excellent companion for genuine enthusiasts, students and professional practitioners of the San Yuan Qi Men Xuan Kong Da Gua studies.

Xuan Kong Collection

Xuan Kong Flying Stars

This book is an essential introductory book to the subject of Xuan Kong Fei Xing, a well-known and popular system of Feng Shui. Learn 'tricks of the trade' and 'trade secrets' to enhance and maximise Qi in your home or office.

Xuan Kong Nine Life Star Series (Available in English & Chinese versions)

Joey Yap's Feng Shui Essentials - The Xuan Kong Nine Life Star Series of books comprises of nine individual titles that provide detailed information about each individual Life Star.

Based on the complex and highly-evolved Xuan Kong Feng Shui system, each book focuses on a particular Life Star and provides you with a detailed Feng Shui guide.

www.masteryacademy.com | +6(03) - 2284 8080

Joey Yap's BaZi Profiling System

Three Levels of BaZi Profiling (English & Chinese versions)

In BaZi Profiling, there are three levels that reflect three different stages of a person's personal nature and character structure.

Level 1 – The Day Master

The Day Master in a nutshell is the basic you. The inborn personality. It is your essential character. It answers the basic question "who am I". There are ten basic personality profiles – the ten Day Masters – each with its unique set of personality traits, likes and dislikes.

Level 2 – The Structure

The Structure is your behavior and attitude – in other words, it is about how you use your personality. It expands on the Day Master (Level 1). The structure reveals your natural tendencies in life – are you a controller, creator, supporter, thinker or connector? Each of the Ten Day Masters express themselves differently through the five Structures. Why do we do the things we do? Why do we like the things we like? The answers are in our BaZi Structure.

Level 3 – The Profile

The Profile depicts your role in your life. There are ten roles (Ten BaZi Profiles) related to us. As to each to his or her own - the roles we play are different from one another and it is unique to each Profile.

What success means to you, for instance, differs from your friends – this is similar to your sense of achievement or whatever you think of your purpose in life is.

Through the BaZi Profile, you will learn the deeper level of your personality. It helps you become aware of your personal strengths and works as a trigger for you to make all the positive changes to be a better version of you.

Keep in mind, only through awareness that you will be able to maximise your natural talents, abilities and skills. Only then, ultimately, you will get to enter into what we refer as 'flow' of life – a state where you have the powerful force to naturally succeed in life.

www.BaZiprofiling.com

THE BaZi
60 PILLARS SERIES

The BaZi 60 Pillars Series is a collection of ten volumes focusing on each of the Pillars or Jia Zi in BaZi Astrology. Learn how to see BaZi Chart in a new light through the Pictorial Method of BaZi analysis and elevate your proficiency in BaZi studies through this new understanding. Joey Yap's 60 Pillars Life Analysis Method is a refined and enhanced technique that is based on the fundamentals set by the true masters of olden times, and modified to fit to the sophistication of current times.

BaZi Collection

With these books, leading Chinese Astrology Master Trainer Joey Yap makes it easy to learn how to unlock your Destiny through your BaZi. BaZi or Four Pillars of Destiny is an ancient Chinese science which enables individuals to understand their personality, hidden talents and abilities, as well as their luck cycle - by examining the information contained within their birth data.

Understand and learn more about this accurate ancient science with this BaZi Collection.

BOOK 1   BOOK 2   BOOK 3   BOOK 4   BOOK 5   The 10 Gods

(Available in English & Chinese)

www.masteryacademy.com | +6(03) - 2284 8080

Feng Shui Collection

Design Your Legacy

Design Your Legacy is Joey Yap's first book on the profound subject of Yin House Feng Shui, which is the study Feng Shui for burials and tombs. Although it is still pretty much a hidden practice that is largely unexplored by modern literature, the significance of Yin House Feng Shui has permeated through the centuries – from the creation of the imperial lineage of emperors in ancient times to the iconic leaders who founded modern China.

This book unveils the true essence of Yin House Feng Shui with its significant applications that are unlike the myths and superstition which have for years, overshadowed the genuine practice itself. Discover how Yin House Feng Shui – the true precursor to all modern Feng Shui practice, can be used to safeguard the future of your descendants and create a lasting legacy.

Must-Haves for Property Analysis!

For homeowners, those looking to build their own home or even investors who are looking to apply Feng Shui to their homes, these series of books provides valuable information from the classical Feng Shui therioes and applications.

In his trademark straight-to-the-point manner, Joey shares with you the Feng Shui do's and dont's when it comes to finding a property with favorable Feng Shui, which is condusive for home living.

Stories and Lessons on Feng Shui Series

(Available in English & Chinese)

All in all, this series is a delightful chronicle of Joey's articles, thoughts and vast experience - as a professional Feng Shui consultant and instructor - that have been purposely refined, edited and expanded upon to make for a light-hearted, interesting yet educational read. And with Feng Shui, BaZi, Mian Xiang and Yi Jing all thrown into this one dish, there's something for everyone.

More Titles under Joey Yap Books

Pure Feng Shui

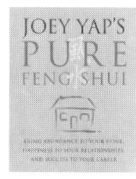

Pure Feng Shui is Joey Yap's debut with an international publisher, CICO Books. It is a refreshing and elegant look at the intricacies of Classical Feng Shui - now compiled in a useful manner for modern day readers. This book is a comprehensive introduction to all the important precepts and techniques of Feng Shui practices.

Your Aquarium Here

This book is the first in Fengshuilogy Series, which is a series of matter-of-fact and useful Feng Shui books designed for the person who wants to do a fuss-free Feng Shui.

More Titles under Joey Yap Books

Walking the Dragons

Compiled in one book for the first time from Joey Yap's Feng Shui Mastery Excursion Series, the book highlights China's extensive, vibrant history with astute observations on the Feng Shui of important sites and places. Learn the landform formations of Yin Houses (tombs and burial places), as well as mountains, temples, castles and villages.

Walking the Dragons : Taiwan Excursion

A Guide to Classical Landform Feng Shui of Taiwan

From China to Tibet, Joey Yap turns his analytical eye towards Taiwan in this extensive Walking the Dragons series. Combined with beautiful images and detailed information about an island once known as Formosa, or "Beautiful Island" in Portuguese, this compelling series of essays highlights the colourful history and wonders of Taiwan. It also provides readers with fascinating insights into the living science of Feng Shui.

The Art of Date Selection: Personal Date Selection (Available in English & Chinese)

With the Art of Date Selection: Personal Date Selection, you can learn simple, practical methods to select not just good dates, but personalised good dates as well. Whether it is a personal activity such as a marriage or professional endeavour, such as launching a business - signing a contract or even acquiring assets, this book will show you how to pick the good dates and tailor them to suit the activity in question, and to avoid the negative ones too!

Your Head Here

Your Head Here is the first book by Sherwin Ng. She is an accomplished student of Joey Yap, and an experienced Feng Shui consultant and instructor with Joey Yap Consulting Group and Mastery Academy respectively. It is the second book under the Fengshuilogy series, which focuses on Bedroom Feng Shui, a specific topic dedicated to optimum bed location and placement.

If the Shoe Fits

This book is for those who want to make the effort to enhance their relationship.

In her debut release, Jessie Lee humbly shares with you the classical BaZi method of the Ten Day Masters and the combination of a new profiling system developed by Joey Yap, to understand and deal with the people around you.

Being Happy and Successful at Work and in your Career

Have you ever wondered why some of us are so successful in our careers while others are dragging their feet to work or switching from one job to another? Janet Yung hopes to answer this question by helping others through the knowledge and application of BaZi and Chinese Astrology. In her debut release, she shares with the readers the right way of using BaZi to understand themselves: their inborn talents, motivations, skills, and passions, to find their own place in the path of professional development.

Being Happy & Successful - Managing Yourself & Others

Manage Your Talent & Have Effective Relationships at the Workplace

While many strive for efficiency in the workplace, it is vital to know how to utilize your talents. In this book, Janet Yung will take you further on how to use the BaZi profiling system as a tool to assess your personality and understanding your approach to the job. From ways in communicating with your colleagues to understanding your boss, you will be astounded by what this ancient system can reveal about you and the people in your life. Tips and guidance will also be given in this book so that you will make better decisions for your next step in advancing in your career.

The BaZi Road to Success

The BaZi Road to Success explains your journey in life through a chart that is obtained just from looking at the date you were born and its connection with key BaZi elements.

Your Day Pillar, Hour Pillar, Luck Pillar and Annual Pillar all come together to paint a BaZi chart that churns out a combination of different elements, which the book helps interpret. From relationships, career advice, future plans and possibility of wealth accumulation - this book covers it all!

Face Reading Collection

The Chinese Art of Face Reading: The Book of Moles

The Book of Moles by Joey Yap delves into the inner meanings of moles and what they reveal about the personality and destiny of an individual. Complemented by fascinating illustrations and Joey Yap's easy-to-understand commentaries and guides, this book takes a deeper focus into a Face Reading subject, which can be used for everyday decisions – from personal relationships to professional dealings and many others.

Discover Face Reading (Available in English & Chinese)

This is a comprehensive book on all areas of Face Reading, covering some of the most important facial features, including the forehead, mouth, ears and even philtrum above your lips. This book will help you analyse not just your Destiny but also help you achieve your full potential and achieve life fulfillment.

Joey Yap's Art of Face Reading

The Art of Face Reading is Joey Yap's second effort with CICO Books, and it takes a lighter, more practical approach to Face Reading. This book does not focus on the individual features as it does on reading the entire face. It is about identifying common personality types and characters.

Faces of Fortune 2

We don't need to go far to look for entrepreneurs with the X-Factor. Malaysia produces some of the best entrepreneurs in the world. In this book, we will tell you the rags-to-riches stories of 9 ordinary people who has no special privileges, and how they made it on their own.

Easy Guide on Face Reading (Available in English & Chinese)

The Face Reading Essentials series of books comprises of five individual books on the key features of the face – the Eyes, the Eyebrows, the Ears, the Nose, and the Mouth. Each book provides a detailed illustration and a simple yet descriptive explanation on the individual types of the features.

The books are equally useful and effective for beginners, enthusiasts and those who are curious. The series is designed to enable people who are new to Face Reading to make the most out of first impressions and learn to apply Face Reading skills to understand the personality and character of their friends, family, co-workers and business associates.

2020 Annual Releases

| Chinese Astrology for 2020 | Feng Shui for 2020 | Tong Shu Desktop Calendar 2020 | Daily Wall Calendar 2020 | Professional Tong Shu Diary 2020 | Tong Shu Monthly Planner 2020 | Weekly Tong Shu Diary 2020 |

Cultural Series

Discover the True Significance of the Ancient Art of Lion Dance

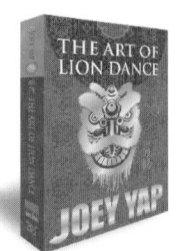

The Lion has long been a symbol of power and strength. That powerful symbol has evolved into an incredible display of a mixture of martial arts and ritualism that is the Lion Dance. Throughout ancient and modern times, the Lion Dance has stamped itself as a popular part of culture, but is there a meaning lost behind this magnificent spectacle?

The Art of Lion Dance written by the world's number one man in Chinese Metaphysics, Dato' Joey Yap, explains the history and origins of the art and its connection to Qi Men Dun Jia. By creating that bridge with Qi Men, the Lion Dance is able to ritualise any type of ceremony, celebrations and mourning alike.

The book is the perfect companion to the modern interpretation of the art as it reveals the significance behind each part of the Lion costume, as well as rituals that are put in place to bring the costume and its spectacle to life.

Chinese Traditions & Practices

China has a long, rich history spanning centuries. As Chinese culture has evolved over the centuries, so have the country's many customs and traditions. Today, there's a Chinese custom for just about every important event in a person's life – from cradle to the grave.

Although many China's customs have survived to the present day, some have been all but forgotten: rendered obsolete by modern day technology. This book explores the history of Chinese traditions and cultural practices, their purpose, and the differences between the traditions of the past and their modern incarnations.

If you are a westerner or less informed about Chinese culture, you may find this book particularly useful, especially when it comes to doing business with the Chinese – whether it be in China itself or some other country with a considerable Chinese population. If anything, it will allow you to have a better casual understanding of the culture and traditions of your Chinese friends or acquaintances. An understanding of Chinese traditions leads to a more informed, richer appreciation of Chinese culture and China itself.

Educational Tools and Software

Joey Yap's Feng Shui Template Set

Directions are the cornerstone of any successful Feng Shui audit or application. The Joey Yap Feng Shui Template Set is a set of three templates to simplify the process of taking directions and determining locations and positions, whether it is for a building, a house, or an open area such as a plot of land - all of it done with just a floor plan or area map.

The Set comprises three basic templates: The Basic Feng Shui Template, Eight Mansions Feng Shui Template, and the Flying Stars Feng Shui Template.

Mini Feng Shui Compass

The Mini Feng Shui Compass is a self-aligning compass that is not only light at 100gms but also built sturdily to ensure it will be convenient to use anywhere. The rings on the Mini Feng Shui Compass are bilingual and incorporate the 24 Mountain Rings that is used in your traditional Luo Pan.

The comprehensive booklet included with this, will guide you in applying the 24 Mountain Directions on your Mini Feng Shui Compass effectively and the Eight Mansions Feng Shui to locate the most auspicious locations within your home, office and surroundings. You can also use the Mini Feng Shui Compass when measuring the direction of your property for the purpose of applying Flying Stars Feng Shui.

MASTERY ACADEMY OF CHINESE METAPHYSICS

Your **Preferred** Choice to the Art & Science of Classical Chinese Metaphysics Studies

Bringing **innovative** techniques and **creative** teaching methods to an ancient study.

Mastery Academy of Chinese Metaphysics was established by Joey Yap to play the role of disseminating this Eastern knowledge to the modern world with the belief that this valuable knowledge should be accessible to everyone and everywhere.

Its goal is to enrich people's lives through accurate, professional teaching and practice of Chinese Metaphysics knowledge globally. It is the first academic institution of its kind in the world to adopt the tradition of Western institutions of higher learning - where students are encouraged to explore, question and challenge themselves, as well as to respect different fields and branches of studies. This is done together with the appreciation and respect of classical ideas and applications that have stood the test of time.

The Art and Science of Chinese Metaphysics – be it Feng Shui, BaZi (Astrology), Qi Men Dun Jia, Mian Xiang (Face Reading), ZeRi (Date Selection) or Yi Jing – is no longer a field shrouded with mystery and superstition. In light of new technology, fresher interpretations and innovative methods, as well as modern teaching tools like the Internet, interactive learning, e-learning and distance learning, anyone from virtually any corner of the globe, who is keen to master these disciplines can do so with ease and confidence under the guidance and support of the Academy.

It has indeed proven to be a centre of educational excellence for thousands of students from over thirty countries across the world; many of whom have moved on to practice classical Chinese Metaphysics professionally in their home countries.

At the Academy, we believe in enriching people's lives by empowering their destinies through the disciplines of Chinese Metaphysics. Learning is not an option - it is a way of life!

MASTERY ACADEMY OF CHINESE METAPHYSICS™

MALAYSIA
19-3, The Boulevard, Mid Valley City, 59200 Kuala Lumpur, Malaysia
Tel : +6(03)-2284 8080 | Fax : +6(03)-2284 1218
Email   : info@masteryacademy.com
Website : www.masteryacademy.com

Australia, Austria, Canada, China, Croatia, Cyprus, Czech Republic, Denmark, France, Germany, Greece, Hungary, India, Italy, Kazakhstan, Malaysia, Netherlands (Holland), New Zealand, Philippines, Poland, Russian Federation, Singapore, Slovenia, South Africa, Switzerland, Turkey, United States of America, Ukraine, United Kingdom

The Mastery Academy around the world!

www.masteryacademy.com | +6(03) - 2284 8080

Feng Shui Mastery™
LIVE COURSES (MODULES ONE TO FOUR)

This an ideal program for those who wants to achieve mastery in Feng Shui from the comfort of their homes. This comprehensive program covers the foundation up to the advanced practitioner levels, touching upon the important theories from various classical Feng Shui systems including Ba Zhai, San Yuan, San He and Xuan Kong.

Module One:	Module Two:	Module Three:	Module Four:
Beginners Course	Practitioners Course	Advanced Practitioners Course	Master Course

BaZi Mastery™
LIVE COURSES (MODULES ONE TO FOUR)

This lesson-based program brings a thorough introduction to BaZi and guides the student step-by-step, all the way to the professional practitioner level. From the theories to the practical, BaZi students along with serious Feng Shui practitioners, can master its application with accuracy and confidence.

Module One:	Module Two:	Module Three:	Module Four:
Intensive Foundation Course	Practitioners Course	Advanced Practitioners Course	Master Course in BaZi

Xuan Kong Mastery™
LIVE COURSES (MODULES ONE TO THREE)
* Advanced Courses For Master Practitioners

Xuan Kong is a sophisticated branch of Feng Shui, replete with many techniques and formulae, which encompass numerology, symbology and the science of the Ba Gua, along with the mathematics of time. This program is ideal for practitioners looking to bring their practice to a more in-depth level.

 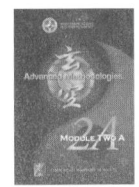  

Module One:	Module Two A:	Module Two B:	Module Three:
Advanced Foundation Course	Advanced Xuan Kong Methodologies	Purple White	Advanced Xuan Kong Da Gua

www.masteryacademy.com | +6(03) - 2284 8080

Mian Xiang Mastery™
LIVE COURSES (MODULES ONE AND TWO)

This program comprises of two modules, each carefully developed to allow students to familiarise with the fundamentals of Mian Xiang or Face Reading and the intricacies of its theories and principles. With lessons guided by video lectures, presentations and notes, students are able to understand and practice Mian Xiang with greater depth.

Module One:
Basic Face Reading

Module Two:
Practical Face Reading

Yi Jing Mastery™
LIVE COURSES (MODULES ONE AND TWO)

Whether you are a casual or serious Yi Jing enthusiast, this lesson-based program contains two modules that brings students deeper into the Chinese science of divination. The lessons will guide students on the mastery of its sophisticated formulas and calculations to derive answers to questions we pose.

Module One:
Traditional Yi Jing

Module Two:
Plum Blossom Numerology

Ze Ri Mastery™
LIVE COURSES (MODULES ONE AND TWO)

In two modules, students will undergo a thorough instruction on the fundamentals of ZeRi or Date Selection. The comprehensive program covers Date Selection for both Personal and Feng Shui purposes to Xuan Kong Da Gua Date Selection.

Module One:
Personal and Feng Shui Date Selection

Module Two:
Xuan Kong Da Gua Date Selection

Joey Yap's
SAN YUAN QI MEN XUAN KONG DA GUA™

This is an advanced level program which can be summed up as the Integral Vision of San Yuan studies – an integration of the ancient potent discipline of Qi Men Dun Jia and the highly popular Xuan Kong 64 Hexagrams. Often regarded as two independent systems, San Yuan Qi Men and San Yuan Xuan Kong Da Gua can trace their origins to the same source and were actually used together in ancient times by great Chinese sages.

This method enables practitioners to harness the Qi of time and space, and predict the outcomes through a highly-detailed analysis of landforms, places and sites.

www.masteryacademy.com | +6(03) - 2284 8080

BaZi 10X

Emphasising on the practical aspects of BaZi, this programme is rich with numerous applications and techniques pertaining to the pursuit of wealth, health, relationship and career, all of which constitute the formula of success. This programme is designed for all levels of practitioners and is supplemented with innovative learning materials to enable easy learning. Discover the different layers of BaZi from a brand new perspective with BaZi 10X.

Feng Shui for Life

This is an entry-level five-day course designed for the Feng Shui beginner to learn the application of practical Feng Shui in day-to-day living. Lessons include quick tips on analysing the BaZi chart, simple Feng Shui solutions for the home, basic Date Selection, useful Face Reading techniques and practical Water formulas. A great introduction course on Chinese Metaphysics studies for beginners.

Joey Yap's Design Your Destiny

This is a three-day life transformation program designed to inspire awareness and action for you to create a better quality of life. It introduces the DRT™ (Decision Referential Technology) method, which utilises the BaZi Personality Profiling system to determine the right version of you, and serves as a tool to help you make better decisions and achieve a better life in the least resistant way possible, based on your Personality Profile Type.

Millionaire Feng Shui Secrets Programme

This program is geared towards maximising your financial goals and dreams through the use of Feng Shui. Focusing mainly on the execution of Wealth Feng Shui techniques such as Luo Shu sectors and more, it is perfect for boosting careers, businesses and investment opportunities.

Grow Rich With BaZi Programme

This comprehensive programme covers the foundation of BaZi studies and presents information from the career, wealth and business standpoint. This course is ideal for those who want to maximise their wealth potential and live the life they deserve. Knowledge gained in this course will be used as driving factors to encourage personal development towards a better future.

Walk the Mountains!
Learn Feng Shui in a Practical and Hands-on Program

 ## Feng Shui Mastery Excursion™

Learn landform (Luan Tou) Feng Shui by walking the mountains and chasing the Dragon's vein in China. This program takes the students in a study tour to examine notable Feng Shui landmarks, mountains, hills, valleys, ancient palaces, famous mansions, houses and tombs in China. The excursion is a practical hands-on course where students are shown to perform readings using the formulas they have learnt and to recognise and read Feng Shui Landform (Luan Tou) formations.

Read about the China Excursion here:
http://www.fengshuiexcursion.com

Mastery Academy courses are conducted around the world. Find out when will Joey Yap be in your area by visiting
www.masteryacademy.com
or call our offices at **+6(03)-2284 8080**.